JEWISH PETITIONARY PRAYER

A Theological Exploration

JEWISH PETITIONARY PRAYER

A Theological Exploration

Dan Cohn-Sherbok

Toronto Studies in Theology
Volume 35

The Edwin Mellen Press
Lewiston●Queenston
Lampeter

Library of Congress Cataloging-in-Publication Data

Dan Cohn-Sherbok
Jewish petitionary prayer.

   (Toronto studies in theology ; v. 35)
   Includes bibliographical references.
   1. Prayer (Judaism) I. Title. II. Title: Petitionary prayer. III. Series.
BM669.C64 1988   296.7'2   88-9256
ISBN 0-88946-781-1

This is volume 35 in the continuing series
Toronto Studies in Theology
Volume 35 ISBN 0-88946-781-1
TST Series ISBN 0-88946-975-X

The Edwin Mellen Press
Box 450
Lewiston, NY
USA 14092

The Edwin Mellen Press
Box 67
Queenston, Ontario
CANADA L0S 1L0

Mellen House
Lampeter, Dyfed, Wales
UNITED KINGDOM SA48 7DY

Printed in the United States of America

TABLE OF CONTENTS

JEWISH PETITIONARY PRAYER

A Theological Exploration

CHAPTER I

INTRODUCTION

Throughout history religious believers have expressed their joys, their sorrows, and their hopes through prayer. Sometimes they have prayed to one god, sometimes to many; sometimes they have prayed when they were not even certain there was anyone to pray to. Prayer is a basic human experience; it is, in the words of F. Heiler, "a living relation of man to God, direct and inner contact, a refuge, a mutual intercourse, a conversation, spiritual commerce, an association, a fellowship, a communion, a converse, a one-ness, a union of an 'I' and a 'thou'...."[1] Essentially prayer falls into four basic categories: praise, thanksgiving, acknowledgement, and petition. Although these four types of prayers are different, they presuppose the existence of a divine reality distinct from the believer who is praying; prayer is not a self-contained activity, rather a dialogue.

In this study I will only be concerned with the fourth kind of prayer, the prayer of petition. This is not to say that I disregard the other kinds of prayer. If there is a God at all, it certainly makes sense to praise, to acknowledge, and to thank Him. Petitionary prayer is another matter altogether and from a philosophical and theological point of view is the most interesting and perplexing type of prayer. Every time an individual asks God for something he is making certain assumptions. Of course as with any prayer there is the assumption that there is a God, but there is more to it than this. Any petitionary prayer takes it for granted that God can and does act as a causal agent. There would be no point in asking for God's help if you did not believe that God could and in fact does act in the world. If an individual makes a request

---

[1] F. Heiler: Prayer, London, Oxford University Press, 1932, p. 357.

because he desires God to grant it, then it only makes sense to assume that he believes that God can and sometimes does fulfil such requests. Yet there are serious problems connected with petitionary prayer. In this study, in which I will refer to the views of both non-Jewish and Jewish writers, I will confine my attention to problems connected with Jewish petitionary prayers. Of course such an investigation overlaps with an analysis of the concept of petitionary prayer in the two other major monotheistic religions (Islam and Christianity) but for reasons of size, scope and personal interest such a limitation is necessary.

Essentially the problems connected with the concept of petitionary prayer concern its objective rather than subjective validity. If a mother prays for her son to survive an airplane crash, obviously the prayer may in some psychological way help her. Prayer often gives strength to the person who prays and comfort to those being prayed for; there can be no dispute about this. What I am trying to discover is whether petitionary prayer has any objective validity. We may at a very simple level ask what sense there is in petitioning God since by His omniscience He already knows all our needs and indeed all that is coming to pass in our world. If God is omnipotent and all-good, it seems that petitonary prayer is superfluous. If all is purposed for good according to God's will, then what reason is there for human beings to tell their needs to God, let alone instruct Him in what He should do? If for example God in His omniscience, omnipotence and goodness had already resolved to destroy Sodom,[2] what point was there for Abraham telling Him of the inhabitants of the city and seeking to change His decision? On the contrary, it would seem that if God knew everything about the city and planned its destruction in His justice, then Abraham's decision would necessarily have been without effect. Furthermore if God had known and determined

---

2   Genesis 18:23-33.

what would happen before Abraham made his petition, then it would have been incompatible with the constancy of the Omnipotent for Abraham's individual entreaty to swing God from His purpose. In this regard we might ask how it would be possible for petitionary prayer to change God's will if in principle God is unchangeable. St. Thomas Aquinas expressed this objection as follows: "By prayer we bend the mind of the person to whom we pray, so that he may do what is asked of him. But God's mind is unchangeable and inflexible.... Therefore, it is not fitting that we should pray to God."[3]

It might be objected also that petitionary prayer is unbecoming since in the words of Aquinas, "it is more liberal to give to one that asks not, than to one who asks"; and he added, since "God is supremely liberal, therefore, it would seem unbecoming to pray to God."[4] This objection is particularly serious with regard to Jewish prayer since the act of petitioning God is a Divine commandment. The Jew is commanded by divinely ordained law to petition God in his personal prayers as well as in the formal services which occur three times daily and on holidays and festivals. For Jews to refrain from praying is to render themselves worthy of punishment. Yet it does seem that it would have been more generous of God to have provided for men's needs without demanding their vocal expression to Him. Furthermore it could be argued that prayers addressed to God freely and spontaneously are preferable to petitionary prayers made in obedience to His commandments.

There are other equally serious difficulties connected with petitionary prayer. We might for example question the fairness

---

[3] St. Thomas Aquinas: Summa Theologica, New York, McGraw Hill, 1963, vol. 39, pp. 50-51. See V. Brummer What Are We Doing When We Pray? London SCM Press, 1984, in which he attempts to escape from these difficulties by redefining omniscience.

[4] Ibid.

of allowing someone to benefit because a prayer has been uttered by them or on their behalf. In this regard H.D. Lewis asks, "Ought not God to benefit men according to their needs or merits and not in terms of the rather haphazard and arbitrary condition of being the subject of prayer? Should momentous things like recovery from sickness, depend on someone's asking God? Will not God, if He has the nature we ascribe to Him, succour men without waiting to be asked?"[5] Does it seem reasonable for example that God would have needed Amos' supplication in order to repent and change his decree concerning the destruction of Israel by her enemies?[6] On the contrary, it would seem that such a momentous event as the destruction of Israel should not, indeed could not, turn on Amos' request to God. It would seem that Amos' praying for Israel or his neglecting to do so is so far removed from the normal necessary and sufficient conditions for the survival and welfare of Israel as to be virtually irrelevant. For Amos to help his fellow Israelites is one thing, to allow their fortunes to depend on whether Amos prays for them or not is another.

Such objections as these raise serious problems touching the reality of evil. From our everyday experiences we know that evil exists in a multitude of forms: pain, suffering, injustice, and sickness are obvious elements of human life. In Dialogues Concerning Natural Religion David Hume eloquently described mankind's universal recognition of such evils. "These miseries of life," he wrote, "the unhappiness of man, the general corruptions of our nature, the unsatisfactory enjoyment of pleasures, riches, honours - these phrases have become almost proverbial in all languages. And who can doubt of what all men

---

[5]   H.D. Lewis: Our Experience of God, London, Allen & Unwin, 1959, p. 251.

[6]   Amos 7: 2-3.

declare from their own immediate feeling and experience?"[7] From the examples of petitionary prayers cited, it is clear that such prayers not only recognise the existence of evil but consciously cry for its irradiation. For example when Rabbi prayed: "May it be Thy will, O Lord our God, and God of our fathers to deliver us from the impudent and from impudence, from an evil man, from evil happenings, from the evil impulse, from an evil companion...," or when we read in the Amidah: "Send perfect healing from our every illness,"[8] these prayers were addressed to God in the hope that they might be effective in securing the elimination of the evil which they mentioned. Yet if God is omnipotent and all-good, why has he allowed a situation to come to be in which prayers need to be offered to Him for such evil to be removed? Indeed how can an omnipotent and all-good God have allowed evil to exist in the first place? These questions were succinctly formulated by Hume in the Dialogues: "Is he [God] willing to prevent evil, but not able? Then he is impotent. Is he able but not willing? Then he is malevolent. Is he both able and willing? Whence then is evil?"[9] We can see then that the classical theological problem concerning the existence of evil is intimately connected with Jewish petitionary prayer.

Another crucial problem of a different order concerning petitionary prayer relates to the criteria we could employ to determine whether or not our petitionary prayers have been efficacious. We might believe that God has answered our prayers affirmatively and has granted our petition, yet how can

---

[7] D. Hume: Dialogues Concerning Natural Religion, New York and London, Hafner Publishing Co., 1969, p. 61.

[8] D. De Sola Pool (Ed.): The Traditional Prayer Book, New York and London, Hafner Publishing Co., 1969, p. 61.

[9] D. Hume: Dialogues Concerning Natural Religion, p. 66. See also E. Stump: 'Petitionary Prayer,' American Philosophical Quarterly, 16, 1979, pp. 81-91.

we in fact know that just this has happened? What sort of evidence have we? Or does our claim rest on an appeal to other considerations independently known such as divine authority? For example when fire had kindled the burnt offering in response to Elijah's petition,[10] how could he have known that this happened in answer to his prayer? One answer to this question is to identify whatever happens with the proper answer to petitionary prayer.[11] If for example Elijah prayed for fire to kindle the burnt offering and fire did in fact come, then on the basis of this view his prayer was answered. But although the kindling of the wood is a necessary condition for Elijah's prayer to have any claim to efficaciousness, it is not sufficient to establish that claim. The fact that fire came does not prove that it was sent by God in answer to Elijah's prayer. If however Elijah had prayed for fire and fire had not come, the devout would insist that his prayer had been answered. The answer would have been negative, a very proper answer to his supplication. In that case we must ask how we could be certain that God had actually considered Elijah's request and answered him negatively. What evidence could be cited in support of such a view? Is it not possible that fire came in answer to his prayer because the latter was unheard, with maybe no one to respond to it?

Another way of trying to escape from this difficulty concerning the grounds for determining whether prayers have been answered is to argue that the only prayers which could be efficacious are those for spiritual benefits such as repentance, the will to perform God's commandments, and so forth. But as H.D. Lewis notes, "however [important] it may be to make these matters uppermost in our prayers, that does not help us at this point. For even if we did hold that the efficacy of prayer was

---

10   I Kings 18: 36-38.

11   H.D. Lewis: Our Experience of God, p. 255.

restricted to spiritual matters... the initial difficulty would present itself quite as formidably at this level as at any other. The evidence might be more elusive, but it is evidence that we should need; something would 'have to be different'."[12]

We must therefore ask in this regard what requirements must a petitionary prayer fulfil in order to be acceptable. Or to put the question differently, are there any types of prayers which could in principle be rejected as unacceptable petitionary prayers? Such prayers as the fourth benediction of the Amidah: "Be pleased to grant us from Thee knowledge, understanding, and discernment"[13] and the eighth benediction of the Amidah: "Heal us, O Lord, and we shall be healed"[14] seem at face value to be not only acceptable but desirable since they are prayers for human welfare and are consonant with God's moral nature. But what about prayers which ask God to perform actions which are not consonant with His nature? If for example I petition God to punish unwarrantably someone I do not like, is such a prayer unacceptable because I am asking God who is all-good to perform an unjust action? Or to take a different case, are prayers which petition God to perform actions which are logically impossible unacceptable in principle? For example if I petition God to change the past, is such a prayer unacceptable? If I had just been in an automobile accident, I might pray, "Please, God, let the accident never have taken place!" Here I would be asking God to perform an act which contains an internal self-contradiction (i.e. create a situation in which an event has both taken and not taken place), and we would have to ask whether God can do such a thing.

Or furthermore, we could ask whether prayers for God to bring about miraculous events are in principle unacceptable. I

---

12   Ibid., p. 256.

13   D. De Sola (Ed.): The Traditional Prayer Book, p. 12.

14   Ibid.

might for example petition God to restore a leg which had just been amputated, yet it is possible to argue that such prayers are in principle unacceptable because they ask God to violate the laws of nature. If one did argue in this way, we would have to ask whether such a view could be compatible with a description of God as omnipotent. I mentioned that it would seem at face value that prayers for human welfare are desirable and in principle acceptable. But what if prayers for altruistic results are motivated by selfish and even malicious motives? If for example I pray that a relative in hospital recovers solely because I do not want to bear the burden of financial responsibility for his illness, do we want to say that such a prayer is unacceptable? It is logically acceptable, for logical acceptability has nothing to do with the motive of the person praying. But is it morally acceptable? If it is not, then it seems that we would have to draw the disturbing conclusion that the motive of the person who is praying is more important than the welfare of the person being prayed for.

It will be with problems such as these that this study intends to deal. It may be the case that we will conclude not only that God can fulfil petitionary prayers, but that He frequently does despite all the apparent problems. On the other hand, we may conclude that although God can answer prayer, it is not in fact the case that He does. Or as a third alternative we might decide that given God's nature, He cannot possibly answer prayer. In this investigation I have accepted the view that religious ideas can be discussed rationally. Some theologians want to say that God's attributes and His nature can never be understood since man's comprehension is so limited and God is so great. Such thinkers argue that when God is said to be "good," His goodness bears no resemblance to what human beings mean by goodness since it is so vastly superior. If this is so, then it is not really possible to say anything unequivocally about God. This view may well be what is really the case, but it would imply that we have no justification for performing religiously significant actions or for saying anything meaningful about God.

An example may help to clarify this point: imagine a Jew who was well-versed in Jewish theology. He might believe that it is impossible to have a correct understanding of God's nature and activity. Yet he wants to pray to God. It is difficult to understand how he can do this. What is he praying to? If God is so unlike us that we have no words to describe Him adequately, how can we be sure He hears prayers? How does He act in the world? What kind of relationship does He have with human beings? How can the believer use any of God's attributes in his prayers? If he believes that nothing can be known about God, he can answer none of these questions. But if he cannot answer these questions, how can he justify his praying? Therefore in order to talk about God at all, we must accept that He does in some measure conform to our description. But if in this study, the reader finds conclusions that are uncongenial to him, he always has a let-out. He can always say that God can in no way be pinned down by theological reflection. Yet if he believes this and also prays to God, he will find himself hard-pressed to explain how he justifies performing a religious act which presupposes knowledge about God's nature and activity.

CHAPTER 2

A SELECTION OF JEWISH PETITIONARY PRAYERS

According to H.H. Farmer, "that prayer is essentially a response of man's spirit to the ultimate as personal is shown by the fact that in its most living and spontaneous utterance, alike in its primitive and most exalted forms, it takes the form of petition... the etymology and cognate usages of the word in most languages indicates that if prayer is the heart of religion, then petition is the heart of prayer."[1] On the basis of this view we would be right in expecting petitionary prayers to have played a major role in the religious life of the Jewish people, especially in view of the successive crises and calamities in which they were involved throughout their history. In such situations Jews continually turned to God for assistance.

Thus in the Hebrew Scriptures we find that petitionary prayers are frequently addressed to God. Abraham for example begged God to spare Sodom since he knew that by destroying the entire population He would destroy the righteous as well as the guilty.[2] In answer to this prayer God agreed to rescind his decision to destroy the city if He could find at least ten righteous men.[3] In another passage, Abraham pleaded with God on his own behalf to give him an heir. "O Lord God," he prayed, "what wilt Thou give me, seeing I go hence childless, and that he who shall be the possessor of my house is Eliezer of Damascus?... Behold, to me thou has given no seed...."[4] In answer to this request God assured Abraham that his descendants would be as numerous as the stars: "Look now toward heaven, and count the stars, if Thou be able to count

---

[1]   H.H. Farmer: The World and God, London, Nisbet & Co. Ltd., 1954, p. 129.

[2]   Genesis 18:23-33.

[3]   Genesis 18:32.

[4]   Genesis 15:2-3.

them; and He said to him, "So shall thy seed be."[5]   Later in the Biblical narrative Sarah is described as conceiving a son in her old age,[6] thereby showing that Abraham's prayer for an heir was granted.

At Beth-El Jacob vowed, "If God will be with me, and will keep me in this way that I go, and will give me bread to eat, and raiment to put on... then shall the Lord be my God..."[7] In another passage in Genesis Abraham's servant journeyed to the city of Nahor on Abraham's instructions to find a wife for Isaac.   When he arrived at Nahor, he prayed:"Oh Lord, the God of my master Abraham ... I pray thee... let it come to pass that the girl to whom I shall say, 'Please set down your pitcher so that I may drink,' and she shall say, 'Drink, and I will also water your camels'; let that girl be the one whom you have selected for Isaac."[8]   In answer to this prayer Rebekah appeared and gave water to Abraham's servant and his camels.   Assured that his prayer had been answered, Abraham's servant gave thanks to God.[9]   After Israel had made a golden calf to worship, Moses begged God to forgive them for this sin.   "Oh, this people have sinned a great sin," he prayed, "and have made them a god of gold.   Yet now, if Thou wilt forgive their sin...; and if not, blot me, I pray Thee, out of Thy book which Thou hast written."[10]   In answer to this supplication God said, "Whosoever hath sinned against Me, him will I blot out of My book.   And now go, lead the people unto the place of which I

---

[5]   Genesis 15:5.

[6]   Genesis 21:2.

[7]   Genesis 28:20-21.

[8]   Genesis 24:12-14.

[9]   Genesis 24:26-27.

[10]   Exodus 32:31-32.

have spoken unto thee."[11]   In other passages Moses asked God to show him His glory[12]and begged for some means by which he could demonstrate to Israel that he was a true prophet.[13]

In Joshua 7 God is described as angry with Israel on account of the sin which Achan had committed.   So when about three thousand Israelites went to conquer the city of Ai, their attack was repulsed.[14]   In desperation Joshua prayed to God implicitly asking for His help to defeat Israel's enemies.   "Alas," he said, "wherefore hast Thou at all brought this people over to Jordan, to deliver us into the hand of the Amorites, to cause us to perish?"[15]   In answer to this request God said to Joshua: "Fear not, neither be thou dismayed; take all the people of war with thee, and arise, go up to Ai; see, I have given into thy hand the king of Ai, and his people, and his city, and his land."[16]   Later Joshua pleaded with God to allow the sun and moon to remain fixed in the sky so that he could defeat the Amorites.[17]

In the book of Judges after Samson had been bound by the men of Judah and delivered to the Philistines, the spirit of God descended upon him and he tore the ropes and bands off his arms and hands.   Then with the jawbone of an ass he smote a thousand Philistines.   Afterwards he prayed to God for something to drink: "Thou hast given this great deliverance by the hand of Thy servant; and now shall I die for thirst, and fall

---

11   Exodus 32:33-34.

12   Exodus 33:13.

13   Exodus 4:1-9.

14   Joshua 7:1-6.

15   Joshua 7:7.

16   Joshua 8:1.

17   Joshua 10:12.

into the hands of the uncircumcised?"[18] In answer to Samson's prayer, "God cleaved the hollow place that is in Lehi, and there came water thereout...."[19] In I Samuel Hannah, the wife of Elkanah, grieved because she was barren. Therefore she prayed to God vowing: "O Lord of hosts, if Thou wilt indeed look on the affliction of Thy handmaid, and remember me, and not forget Thy handmaid, but wilt give unto Thy handmaid a manchild, then I will give him unto the Lord all the days of his life...."[20] In response to this prayer God caused Hannah to conceive - she called her son Samuel because, she said, "I have asked him of the Lord."[21]

In the accounts of the prophets again we find examples of petitionary prayers. For example in I Kings 18:20-39 a contest is described between the prophets of Baal and the prophet Elijah. Two bullocks were prepared for sacrifice and placed on pieces of wood and then Elijah declared to the prophets of Baal, "Call ye on the name of your god, and I will call on the name of the Lord; and the God that answereth by fire, let him be God."[22] After the Israelites agreed to this proposal, Elijah prayed for God to send fire to consume the burnt offering: "O Lord, the God of Abraham, of Isaac, and of Israel, let it be known this day that I am Thy servant and that I have done all these things at Thy word. Here me, O Lord, hear me, that this people may know that Thou, Lord, art God...."[23] In response to

---

18   Judges 15:18.

19   Judges 16:19.

20   I Samuel 1:11.

21   I Samuel 1:20.

22   I Kings 18:24.

23   I Kings 18:36-37.

Elijah's prayer, "the fire of the Lord fell, and consumed the burnt-offering, and the wood, and the stones...."[24]

In the prophetic books we find similar instances of such entreaties. Thus in the book of Amos God showed Amos a vision of locusts devouring the grass of the land - a symbol of the destruction of Israel by her enemies.[25] Thereupon Amos prayed to God: "O Lord," he pleaded, "forgive, I beseech Thee; how shall Jacob stand for he is small."[26] In response, "the Lord repented concerning this; 'It shall not be,' said the Lord."[27] Again we find a very different example in the book of Jonah. After the people of Nineveh repented and turned from their evil way, God decided to refrain from destroying the city In anger Jonah addressed God. "I pray Thee, O Lord," he said, "was not this my saying, when I was yet in mine own country? Therefore, I fled beforehand into Tarshish; for I knew that Thou art a gracious God, and compassionate, long-suffering, and abundant in mercy, and repentest Thee of the evil. Therefore now, O Lord, take, I beseech Thee, my life from me; for it is better for me to die than to live."[28] But rather than grant his request God rebuked Jonah for his attitude.[29] In a prayer of a different order Job expressed a similar wish that he had never been born.[30]

In addition to the prayers in the Torah, in the historical, and in the prophetic books (of which I have offered a

---

[24] I Kings 18:38.

[25] Amos 7:1.

[26] Amos 7:2.

[27] Amos 7:3.

[28] Jonah 4:2-3.

[29] Jonah 4:9-11.

[30] Job 3:3.

representative sample) we find numerous forms of petitionary prayers in the Psalms. Various psalmists petitioned God not to rebuke or chasten Israel but rather to be gracious to her and heal her:[31] not to forget the humble;[32] to protect the psalmist from his oppressors;[33] to accept the psalmist's worship;[34] to give guidance and teaching;[35] not to forsake the psalmist;[36] to deliver the psalmist from his enemies;[37] to listen attentively to the psalmist's prayer;[38] to make the psalmist's enemies ashamed and disconcerted;[39] to make the righteous flourish;[40] to give the psalmist strength;[41] and to help the psalmist not to perform any evil action.[42]

After the destruction of the Temple in 70 A.D. prayer took the place of the sacrificial system; thus petitionary prayer played an even more major role in Jewish worship. The Talmud, and in particular the Tractate Berakoth which deals with prayer and worship, records numerous prayers of the sages in which they petitioned God. R. Eleazar for example after finishing the Amidah used to pray, "May it be Thy will, O Lord our God, to

---

[31]   Psalm 6:2.

[32]   Psalm 10:12.

[33]   Psalm 17:8-9.

[34]   Psalm 19:14.

[35]   Psalm 25:5.

[36]   Psalm 38:21.

[37]   Psalm 59:1.

[38]   Psalm 61:1.

[39]   Psalm 70:2.

[40]   Psalm 72:7.

[41]   Psalm 86:16.

[42]   Psalm 141:4.

cause to dwell in our lot love and brotherhood and peace and friendship, and mayest Thou make our borders rich in disciples and prosper our latter end with good prospect and hope; and set our portion in Paradise, and cause us to obtain a good companion and a good impulse in Thy world...."[43]   After concluding the Amidah R. Johanan used to pray: "May it be Thy will, O Lord our God, to look upon our shame, and behold our evil plight, and clothe Thyself with Thy graciousness, and may the attribute of Thy kindness and gentleness come before Thee."[44]   On concluding the last benediction of the Amidah Rabbi used to add, "May it be Thy will, O Lord our God, and God of our fathers, to deliver us from the impudent and from impudence, from an evil man, from evil happenings, from the evil impulse, from an evil companion, from an evil neighbour, and from the destructive accuser, from a hard lawsuit and from a hard opponent, whether he is a son of the covenant or not a son of the covenant."[45]   When Rab finished the Amidah, he added: "May it be Thy will, O Lord our God, to grant us long life, a life of bodily vigour, a life in which there is fear of sin, a life free from shame and confusion, a life of riches and honour, a life in which Thou shalt fulfil all the desires of our heart for good."[46]

These personal prayers of the sages of Israel were added to the fixed liturgy of the synagogue which existed even from the time of the Second Temple.[47]   This liturgical form eventually evolved into the standard Jewish Prayer Book and

---

43   Berakoth 16b.

44   Ibid.

45   Ibid.

46   Ibid.

47   A.Z. Idelsohn: Jewish Liturgy, New York, Schocken, 1967, p. 25.

became the central repository of the prayers of the Jewish people. According to A.Z. Idelsohn, the Prayer Book "is the mirror of the spirit of the Jewish people and its development... this book is the true companion of the Jew from the years of his early youth to the hour of his death. Next to the Bible, it is the most popular book in Jewish life; to a certain extent it is even closer to him, since it was at no time canonized but continued to develop and to reflect the daily occurrences of the Jewish people."[48]   In the words of Phillip Birnbaum, "the whole gamut of Jewish history may be traversed in its [the Prayer Book's] pages.... Interwoven into the texture of its prayers and hymns are passages from the Bible, the Mishnah, the Talmud, and the Zohar.   The poetic and philosophic creations of numerous known and unknown authors constitute an integral part of the Mahzor [Prayer Book]."[49]   It is to the Prayer Book then that we should look for a broad collection of Jewish petitionary prayers.

The Amidah (or Eighteen Benedictions) to which the sages added their personal prayers contains a variety of petitionary prayers.   The Amidah opens with the following petitionary declaration: "Lord, open my lips that my mouth may declare Thy praise."[50]   In the fourth benediction there is a prayer for knowledge and wisdom: "Be pleased to grant from Thee knowledge, understanding, and discernment."[51]   The fifth benediction is a prayer that God cause Israel to return to His law and service: "Our Father and King, cause us to turn to Thy Torah, and draw near to Thy service.   Bring us back through

---

[48]   Ibid. p. xii.

[49]   High Holy Day Prayer Book, New York, Hebrew Publishing Co., 1951, p. xi.

[50]   D. De Sola Pool (Ed.): The Traditional Prayer Book, p. 8.

[51]   Ibid. p. 12.

perfect repentance before Thee."[52]   The sixth benediction is a prayer for forgiveness: "Our Father and King, forgive us that we have sinned, and pardon us that we have transgressed, for Thou art pardoning and forgiving."[53]   The seventh benediction which is based on a petitionary prayer contained in Psalm 119: 153-4[54] is a prayer for redemption: "Behold our affliction and take up our cause. Speed our redemption for the sake of Thy name, for Thou art mighty to redeem." The eighth benediction which is derived from a petitionary prayer in Jeremiah 17:14[55] is a prayer for the sick: "Heal us, O Lord, and we shall be healed; save us and we shall be saved; for Thou art our praise. Send perfect healing from our every illness."[56]   The ninth benediction which was originally an agricultural prayer is a petition for a prosperous year: "Lord our God, bless for us this year and all its varied produce for our welfare." From the winter season on one is required to add to this benediction a prayer for moisture: "Send dew and rain for blessing on the face of the earth."[57] The tenth benediction which is derived from Isaiah 27:13; 11:12 and Ezekiel 20:34; 37:21; 39:2 is a prayer for the gathering of the exiled Jews from their dispersion to Palestine:[58]   "Sound Thou on the great shofar the summons for our freedom; lift up

52   Ibid.

53   Ibid,

54   A.Z. Idesohn: Jewish Liturgy, p. 99.

55   Ibid. p. 100.

56   D. De Sola Pool (Ed.): The Traditional Prayer Book, p. 12.

57   Ibid. pp. 12-14.

58   A.Z. Idesohn: Jewish Liturgy, p. 101.

a banner for the ingathering of our exiles; and bring us together from the four corners of the earth."[59]

The eleventh benediction which is derived from Isaiah 1:26-27[60] is a prayer for the domination of righteous judgement: "Restore our judges as of yore, our counsellors as aforetime, and relieve us from sorrow and distress."[61] The twelfth benediction is a malediction against sectarians and heretics among the Jewish people: "May traducers find no hope, and may all wickedness vanish as in a moment. May all Thine enemies be speedily cut down, and all godless tyrants be uprooted, broken, overthrown, and humbled speedily in our day."[62] The thirteenth benediction is a prayer for the righteous and pious as well as true proselytes and the remnant of the Scribes: "Lord, Our God, let Thy tender mercies flow toward the righteous, the pious, the elders of the house of Israel Thy people, the remnant of their scribes, the true proselytes, and toward us."[63] The fourteenth prayer is a petition for the rebuilding of Jerusalem: "Return with compassion to Jerusalem, Thy city, and dwell therein as Thou hast spoken. Rebuild it soon in our day for all time, and establish soon therein the throne of David."[64] The fifteenth benediction is a prayer for the reinstatement of the dynasty of David: "Cause Thou the scion of Thy servant David soon to flourish, and be his strength exalted through Thy saving

---

[59]   D. De Sola Pool (Ed.): The Traditional Prayer Book, p. 14.

[60]   A.Z. Idesohn: Jewish Liturgy, p. 101.

[61]   D. De Sola Pool (Ed.): The Traditional Prayer Book, p. 14.

[62]   Ibid.

[63]   Ibid.

[64]   Ibid. p. 16.

power..."[65]   The sixteenth prayer which concludes the petitional section of the Amidah is a prayer for God to accept these supplications: "Lord our God, hear our voice, have compassion and pity on us.   Accept our supplication with loving favour, for Thou art God who harkens to plea and prayer.   Send us not far from Thy presence without response, O our King, for Thou hearest the prayer of Thy people Israel in compassion."[66]

In addition to the petitionary prayers contained in the Amidah other petitions are found throughout the Prayer Book. During the morning service for the Sabbath and Festivals for example we read in the silent meditation: "Lord of the universe, fulfil the prayers of my heart for good.   Respond to my desires and answer my prayerful petition.   May it be given to me and to all my family to perform Thy will with a whole heart..... May it be Thy will, Lord our God, God of our fathers, that we be privileged to do deeds that are good in Thy sight and to walk before Thee in the ways of the upright."[67]   In the same morning service for Sabbath and Festivals the following prayer is said for scholars: "May Heaven grant redemption, gracious favour, loving kindness, length of days with ample sustenance, divine support, health of body and spiritual enlightenment, with offspring who will live and will not neglect or give up the study of the Torah, to our teachers and rabbis of the holy communities in all the lands of our dispersion...."[68]   In the Memorial Service for the departed we read the following prayer in memory of a father: "God, be mindful of the soul of my beloved father who has been called to his eternal home.... May his soul be bound up in the bond of life with the souls of

---

65   Ibid.

66   Ibid.

67   Ibid. p. 240.

68   Ibid. p. 256.

Abraham, Isaac, Jacob, Sarah, Rebecca, Rachel, Leah, and all the other righteous ones in eternal bliss."[69]   In the evening service for Yom Kippur we read: "O pardon the iniquities of this people, according to thy abundant kindness, even as thou hast forgiven this people, according to thy abundant kindness, even as thou has forgiven this people ever since they left Egypt."[70]   In the morning service for Yom Kippur we read a similar prayer for forgiveness: "Our God and God of our fathers, may our prayer reach thee: 'Lord our God and God of our fathers, we are just and have not sinned.'   Indeed, we have sinned..... Now may it be thy will, Lord our God and God of our fathers, to forgive all our sins, to pardon our iniquities, and to grant atonement for all our transgressions."[71]

These prayers illustrate the sorts of petitionary prayers met in the Old Testament, Rabbinic sources, and the Jewish Prayer Book.   On the basis of this brief survey we may make three comments:

(1)   Both the form and the content of Jewish petitionary prayers has remained remarkably constant across the centuries. Thus the prayers of the patriarchs closely resemble those of the rabbis and numerous prayers found in the Jewish Prayer Book. This should not surprise us since, as Birnbaum remarked, passages from the Bible as well as rabbinic sources are woven into the texture of the prayers in the Jewish Prayer Book. What is most important is the fact that through millennia of years of social, political, intellectual, and religious development Jews have never wavered in their readiness to turn to God for help and have done so in forms of petition which have not essentially changed.

---

69   Ibid. p. 476.

70   High Holy Day Prayer Book, p. 492.

71   Ibid. pp. 614-616.

(2) From the examples I cited we seem to be able to distinguish three sorts of Jewish petitionary prayers. Firstly we have what I call prayers for tangible objects illustrated by such various examples as Jacob's prayer for food and clothing; Samson's prayer for something to drink; Hannah and Abraham's prayer for a son; Elijah's prayer for fire on Mt. Carmel; Rab's prayer for riches; and the ninth benediction of the Amidah's supplication for rain. Secondly, we may distinguish prayers to God to bring about a change in respect of the psychological, physical, intellectual or religious welfare of an individual or a group. Examples of such prayers are the psalmist's plea to God to be gracious to Israel and heal her rather than rebuke and chasten her, and the psalmist's request for guidance and teaching, for strength in weakness, and for divine help to avoid the guilt of evildoing. With such prayers we may group Rabbi's request to be delivered from an evil inclination and Rab's request for bodily vigour and a life free from shame and confusion. Again it is to this class that I would assign the fourth benediction of the Amidah's supplication for knowledge, understanding and discernment; the eighth benediction of the Amidah's request for healing; and the prayers for forgiveness on Yom Kippur. Finally, I would distinguish prayers for God to bring about or to refrain from bringing about an event. Here one thinks of Abraham's intercession to God on behalf of Sodom; Joshua's prayer for help in defeating the Amorites; Amos' entreaty to God to refrain from destroying Israel; and Jonah's request to God to end his life. In addition we should include the psalmist's frequent requests to be delivered from his enemies; R. Eleazar's request for Israel to be full of disciples; Rabbi's request to be delivered from evil happenings; the tenth benediction of the Amidah's supplication for an ingathering of the exiled Jews to Palestine; and the fourteenth benediction of the Amidah's supplication for the rebuilding of Jerusalem.

Of course such classification is artificial. It is true that if God causes fire to kindle the burnt-offering in answer to Elijah's prayer, the coming of the fire upon the offering is an event. Similarly if God causes rain to fall in answer to prayer, the shower is an event. In these cases the object of prayer is in the one case a kindling of fire, in the other the onset of a shower. When however one prays for strength or for victory in war, the object is much more complex, involving changes in the behaviour of many other people as well as oneself. So these distinctions (as later use of them will show) are helpful in isolating certain problems related to petitionary prayer.

(3) All the prayers cited take for granted that God can and does act as a causal agent in answering the various petitions addressed to Him. This is illustrated by the sorts of Hebrew expressions used in petitionary prayers to supplicate God and to describe His activity. Frequently for example imperatives are used to petition God. (In most cases such imperatives are followed by the particle of entreaty (I pray Thee), but nevertheless such imperatives function primarily as commands or exhortations.) It would only make sense to address imperatives to God if one takes for granted that God could respond to the requests made to Him. For example if one asked God to pay attention to the affliction of Israel, such an exhortation would be futile unless the person who made the exhortation believed that God could do so. Again if one exhorted God to forgive Israel for her sins, the intercessor must believe God can and will forgive Israel. This is a similar principle to the one we apply constantly in ordinary situations. If for example I am in a hot room and say to a friend near the window: "Please open the window" (thereby using the imperative and an adverb and tone of voice calculated to make my desire known), I do so because I know that the person addressed can do so. It would be sheer brutishness as well as futile to make such a request to a chair-bound cripple or to a man with one arm, and that in a

sling. My point is that in similar cases when by means of imperatives we exhort God to fulfil particular requests, we act in this way because we believe that God can in fact do so. In addition to imperatives, causative verbs are frequently used to indicate God's causal action. When we read a petition for God to cause us to turn to His Torah for example, what is clearly meant is that God can influence us. Transitive verbs which take a direct object are also used to describe God's activity in response to petitionary prayer. When God is depicted in these cases as acting in such a way as to have direct effect on an object, God is thereby portrayed as a causal agent in fulfilling the requests made to Him. For example when Jonah petitioned God to take his life, by Jonah's description of God's action he must have believed that God could act as a cause in bringing about his death.

It might be objected however that there are cases in which individuals seem to make requests to God without believing that God can fulfil them, or even without believing that God exists. For example a Jew might be forced to participate in a Jewish worship service because of external pressure (such as the will of his parents or family) and yet not believe that the petitionary prayers he recited could have any effect. But in such cases the individual who makes a request to God would be doing no more than reciting a series of sentences averting from their sense. Rather than praying he would merely be conforming, or showing courtesy to others who would be hurt by his absence. Of course the language of request can be spoken by an atheist; he can go through the motions. But what I am arguing is that if an individual makes a supplication to God because he desires God to fulfil his request, it only makes sense to assume that he believes that God exists and can in fact grant his petition. In summary, we can see from this selection that petitionary prayer has played a major role in the religious life of the Jewish people and is a central element in Jewish worship. Although this sample of prayers is by no means exhaustive, it nevertheless indicates the types of requests Jews have made throughout their history and presently make to God. These prayers as well as similar personal prayers Jews make in their daily lives will serve as the basis for the discussion in the rest of this study.

CHAPTER 3

REDUCTIONISM AND PETITIONARY PRAYERS

In Chapter 2 we saw that the types of expressions used in petitionary prayers to supplicate God and to describe His activity demonstrate that these prayers presuppose that God can act as a causal agent in respect of the various requests addressed to Him. Although this definition and description of petitionary prayers has much to commend it, recent philosophers of religion have offered serious criticisms. Such philosophers argue that the term "petition" when applied to petitionary prayers is used differently from the sorts of use illustrated in ordinary discourse. When we petition God, these philosophers have argued, we are not making a request. According to this view petitionary prayers should be understood as expressions of religious commitment, praise of God, and so forth and must be analyzed from within the religious contexts in which they occur. The most comprehensive attempt to reduce petitionary prayers to other forms of expression is contained in The Concept of Prayer by D.Z. Phillips. "What I want to say of petitionary prayers," he writes "is [that] when deep religious believers pray for something they are not so much asking God to bring this about, but in a way telling Him of the strength of their desires. They realize that things may not go as they wish, but they are asking to be able to go on living whatever happens. In prayers.... of petition, the believer is trying to find a meaning and a hope that will deliver him from the elements which threaten to destroy it."[1]

Certainly when one prays for something, one is not merely telling God what one wants but also testifying to the strength of one's desires. And of course those who pray realize that things may not go as they wish. Indeed such a realization is

---

[1] D.Z. Phillips: The Concept of Prayer, London, Routledge & Kegan Paul, 1965, p. 30.

entailed in the notion of petition. God is so much greater than human beings that it would make no sense to expect that He would necessarily carry out the requests made to Him. Furthermore many believers who petition God may be asking Him to be able to go on living whatever happens, and they might add this supplication to their original petition. One might pray for example, "Please heal me, God. But if it is not in Your divine plan to do so, then please help me to go on living whatever happens." Yet this desire is not necessarily contained in every petitionary prayer. A petitionary prayer is an explicit request for something and unless otherwise indicated not a request to go on living whether the initial request is granted or not. It may be the case that when some believers pray to God, they are searching for such a hope and meaning. But it is not so with every believer; in many if not most cases one who petitions God is simply asking that his request be granted.

One of the main faults of Phillips' analysis of petitionary prayer is that he confuses a recommendation for the use of petitionary prayer with its analysis. Philosophers of religion like Phillips who argue that religious statements are not factual assertions but expressions of religious commitment, loyalty to a particular way of life, etc. fail to realize that they are recommending a use for such statements rather than analyzing the statements themselves. Clearly by means of such religious claims one may express a commitment to a particular religion or way of life; yet preeminently the devout are making assertions about the nature and activity of God which they believe are factually significant. Phillips speaks as if he is saying what petitionary prayer is, as if he is giving an adequate account of what people are doing when they utter petitionary prayers. But in fact all he has done is to explain a particular psychological function of prayer. He is telling us what benefits can be derived from the use of petitionary prayer. If Phillips' depiction of petitionary prayer were correct, then we would need to ask why the believer who utters a petitionary prayer formulates his supplication in the way he does. That is to say, if the person who makes a petitionary prayer is doing no more than asking God to help him to go on living whatever happens, then why does he not say: "God, please help me to go on living whatever happens"? If this is what he is asking, why does he pray instead: "Please, God, grant that such and such takes place"?

It is clear that Phillips' analysis of what people are doing when they utter petitionary prayers does not adequately account for the types of petitionary prayers found in the Bible, Rabbinic literature, and the Jewish Prayer Book. For example when Elijah prayed for fire to kindle a burnt-offering, he was not merely telling God "the strength of his desires" or "asking to be able to go on living whatever happens." Rather he was making an explicit appeal for fire to kindle the burnt offering so that Israelites would worship the God of Israel rather than Baal. It may have been the case that Elijah did pray to God to be able to go on living whether the fire was sent or not. But such a prayer would have been an addition to his original prayer, and it is certainly not found in Scripture. The same holds true for other instances of petitionary prayer in the Bible. When Samson prayed for drink, Hannah prayed for a child, Joshua prayed for victory, and Jacob prayed for food and drink, these supplications were explicit requests to God. They were not prayers which told God the strength of the petitioners' desires nor which asked Him for help to go on living.

In Rabbinic literature when R. Eleazar prayed: "Mayest Thou make our borders rich in disciples,"[2] he was not asking God to help Israel to endure whatever the future. Rather his intention was to request God to increase Israel's borders with disciples. (The fact that R. Eleazar prefaced his prayer with the phrase, "May it be Thy will," does not indicate that his

---

2   Berakoth, 16b.

prayer was no more than an expression of his willingness to accept God's decision. Rather such a phrase was a common formula of entreaty often affixed to petitionary prayers in Rabbinic sources.) The same point also applies to other prayers in Rabbinic sources and in the Jewish Prayer Book. For example Rabbi's prayer to be delivered from evil men, evil happenings and evil neighbours; Rab's prayer for a long life, a life of good, and a life of bodily vigour; and the tenth benediction of the Amidah for the ingathering of the exiled Jews from their dispersion are all explicit requests for God to act. They are not requests for God's help in enduring whatever happens, nor merely expressions of the strength of the petitioners' desires.

Phillips' discussion of petitionary prayer is particularly inadequate when he describes what a petitioner does when he prays for others. According to Phillips, when a missionary asserts, "I depend on your prayers," this "does not refer to dependence on some mysterious form of communication, but rather to the meaning which the knowledge that he is actually being prayed for, or the knowledge that he belongs to a praying community, has for the absent member of the community. This is not a psychological question, but a religious one, in which dependence is seen as dependence on the prayers of the fellow believers."[3] Furthermore, Phillips believes that when a missionary claims that he depends on the prayers of a community, he does not mean that he is depending on an act of God in response to the prayers of the group. Rather he is relying on the goodwill of the community as expressed through their prayers to him. Presumably Phillips thinks that when they are praying for the missionary, the community is not praying for any act of God on his behalf. But we must ask what precisely

---

[3]   D.Z. Phillips: The Concept of Prayer, p. 127.

the community is praying for, and how is the missionary helped by their prayers.

We are told that the fact that the community is praying for the missionary "has meaning" for him. Arguably this means that he gains some sort of moral or spiritual strength from the knowledge that the community is concerned about his welfare. But Phillips also says that the missionary "need not actually know that such prayers are being offered."[4] If this is so, then the prayers cannot "have meaning" for him in the sense that he is strengthened or encouraged by knowing that the community is praying on his behalf. Furthermore as we have seen Phillips does not believe that God acts as a causal agent in response to petitionary prayer. Thus in terms of his account of the nature of petitionary prayer, the community could not be praying that God provide strength and encouragement for the missionary. It would seem then that, in the words of T.P. Smith, "the only effects or results of such prayers must be on the community itself, which amounts to saying that when a community apparently prays for a missionary - or a victim of a disaster or a hospital patient or anyone else - if the person being 'prayed for' does not <u>know</u> that he is being 'prayed for' then, on Phillips' analysis, the community is after all praying for itself (asking to go on living whatever happens), or it is praying for no one at all."[5] But it is absurd to think, as Phillips seems to do, that the community when offering prayers for someone else is in reality praying for itself. What if the missionary learns that the community is praying for him? Does such knowledge have some effect in strengthening and encouraging him? It would seem that it would not since, according to Phillips, the community is really praying for itself - it is difficult to conceive how the missionary could be strengthened or

---

4   <u>Ibid</u>.

5   T.P. Smith: Unpublished Article, p. 40.

encouraged if he learned that the community was praying in this way. Indeed, he might be discouraged if he learned that when the community was ostensibly praying for him, it was not in fact doing so.

There is a further difficulty in Phillips' understanding of what happens when a community or an individual petitions God on behalf of others. Phillips writes that "the prayer of petition is best understood, not as an attempt at influencing the way things go, but as an expression of, and a request for devotion of God through the way things go."[6] In other words, as we noted previously, Phillips believes that the petitioner in offering his petitionary prayer is really only praying to go on living whatever happens. But as D.M. MacKinnon points out,[7] on this view any two petitionary prayers regardless of their formulation are really prayers for the same thing. For example the following two prayers from the Amidah despite their differences are equivalent prayers:

(1)   "Heal us, O Lord, and we shall be healed...."

(2)   "Send dew and rain for blessing on the face of the earth...."

On Phillips' reductionist account, (1) is really the following prayer: "Please help me to go on living whatever happens." But by the same token (2) is really also the same prayer: "Please help me to go on living whatever happens." In other words (1) and (2) say exactly the same thing. Yet it is quite clear that they do not say the same thing at all. T.P. Smith makes just this point: "A prayer of petition might well take the form: "Please grant that p (any proposition), but let me go on living whatever happens." In such a prayer, if Phillips be correct, the second element ('... but let me...') really repeats the first ('Please grant that p'). This too is pretty obviously not what is

---

6   D.Z. Phillips: The Concept of Prayer, pp. 120-121.

7   T.P. Smith: Unpublished Article, p. 46.

happening in such a case. The second element is an addition of the first."[8]

The previous objections brought against Phillips' analysis of petitionary prayer were concerned with the inadequacy of his account. Let us now turn to an objection concerning the logical consistency of his analysis. We have seen that according to Phillips the believer in uttering a petitionary prayer is not really petitioning God but rather informing Him of the strength of his desires and asking God to help him to go on living whatever happens. In addition Phillips asserts that petitionary prayer should be understood as an expression of and a request for devotion to God through the way things go. By such a reduction Phillips hopes to overcome the difficulties inherent in the notion of God acting as a causal agent in response to prayer. But although Phillips is at pains to deny that petitionary prayer presupposes that God acts as a causal agent in the world, his own understanding of petitionary prayer contains just such a belief. If, as Phillips contends, those who utter petitionary prayers are asking to be able to go on living whatever happens, they are in fact asking for something, making a request after all. In the words of H.H. Farmer: "The compromise made by some of not praying for external events to happen, but only praying for the right attitude to whatever events may happen, is only a subterfuge.... For a mental attitude is an event, and, scientifically considered, is as much within the causal nexus of the natural order as any other. To pray to God to change (or preserve) our attitudes is as much a request to bring about something which would not otherwise happen as it is to pray to Him to change the weather."[9] Thus although Phillips assumes that by his analysis of petitionary prayer he is able to remove the notion of "petition" as used in

---

8   Ibid. p. 47.

9   H.H. Farmer: The World and God, p. 136.

ordinary   discourse,   he   only   reintroduces   this   notion   without acknowledging that he is doing so.

Phillips'   discussion   is   the   most   well-known   and comprehensive   reductionist   account   of   petitionary   prayer,   but within   the   Jewish   world   there   have   also   appeared   similar reductionist   interpretations   to   meet   some   of   the   perplexities inherent   in   the   notion   of   making   a   request   to   God.   These Jewish   writers   have   attempted   to   resolve   some   of   the   problems connected   with   petitionary   prayer   which   were   raised   by   medieval Jewish   philosophers.   Jacob Petuchowski   for   example,   in   an   essay entitled   "Can   Modern   Man   Pray?",   quotes   a   passage   from   the Ikkarim   by   the   medievalist   Joseph   Albo   in   which   he   discusses prayers   of   supplication.   According   to   Albo,   "Either   God   has determined   that   a   given   person   shall   receive   a   given   benefit,   or He   has   not   so   determined.   If   he   has   determined,   there   is   no need   of   prayer;   and   if   He   has   not   determined,   how   can   prayer avail   to   change   God's   will   that   He   should   now   determine   to benefit   the   person,   when   he   had   not   so   determined   before?   For God   does   not   change   from   a   state   of   willing   to   a   state   of   not willing   or   vice versa.   For   this   reason   they   say   that   right conduct   is   of   no   avail   for   receiving   a   good   from   God.   And similarly,   they   say   that   prayer   does   not   avail   to   enable   one   to receive   benefit,   or   to   be   saved   from   an   evil   which   has   been decreed   against   him."[10]   In   other   words   Albo   argued   that   if   God has   decided   what   He   is   going   to   do,   then   there   is   no   point   in praying because God is unchangeable.

Petuchowski   admits   that   such   difficulties   are   serious.   "The prayer   of   petition,"   he   writes,   is   "the   most   difficult   form   of prayer   to   justify   theologically...",[11]   but   rather   than   meeting   the criticisms   made   by   Albo   and   others   Petuchowski   attempts   to

---

[10]   J.   Petuchowski   (Ed.):   Understanding   Jewish   Prayer, New York, KTAV, 1972, p. 57.

[11]   Ibid. p. 35.

retreat from these difficulties by offering a reductionist interpretation. "Petitionary prayer," he writes, "as we have seen, is a human need rather than something required by God. God knows our needs before we utter them, and he will do what is good in His sight. But man was afforded an opportunity of rehearsing his wants and his concerns before God. It was the genius of Judaism to turn man's petitionary prayer into a praise of God."[12] Here Petuchowski admits that God knows our needs and provides for us according to what is good in His sight, yet he argues that man is afforded an opportunity to rehearse his wants and concerns before God. Apparently Petuchowski believes that such a rehearsal is in essence a means of praising God. But in what way can petitionary prayers be understood as expressions of praise? At face value they seem utterly different. For example the fourth benediction of the Amidah: "Be pleased to grant us from Thee knowledge, understanding, and discernment," is totally unlike the Kedushah prayer of the Shemoneh Esreh: "Thou art holy, Thy name is holy, and holy ones each day shall praise Thee evermore; blessed art Thou, Lord, the holy God."[13] In the latter case no request is made to God; in the former God is not praised. These prayers serve two entirely different liturgical functions, and thus Petuchowski is mistaken in assuming that prayers of supplication and prayers of praise - regardless of their formulation - say the same thing.

Perhaps what Petuchowski is trying to illustrate is that although petitionary prayers are not explicit statements of praise, they are implicit assertions of man's dependence on God as well as attestations of God's greatness. In this sense they are prayers of praise. For example the petitionary prayer: "Be pleased to grant us from Thee knowledge, understanding and

---

[12] Ibid. p. 42.

[13] D. De Sola Pool (Ed.): The Traditional Prayer Book, p.12.

discernment" emphasizes the fact that God possesses knowledge, understanding and discernment, and that man is dependent on God for obtaining such qualities. In line with this interpretation Aquinas argued that the central purpose of petitionary prayer is to demonstrate man's dependence on God's greatness. "We need to pray to God," he wrote, "not in order to make known to Him our needs or desires, but that we ourselves may be reminded of the necessity of having recourse to God's help in these matters."[14] Nevertheless although petitionary prayers contain implicit assumptions about the nature of God and man, this does not mean that the aim of such prayer is to praise God.

The same holds true of statements we make about everyday events. The fact that these statements contain implicit assumptions about the world does not mean that we are making them explicit and thereby the subject of the statements themselves. For example if I say, "It is snowing outside," this assertion is based on a number of implicit presuppositions about the natural world. But they are not what is being asserted in the statement - what is being said is simply that it is snowing outside. Similarly if I pray, "Be pleased to grant us from Thee knowledge, understanding and discernment," such a prayer makes certain assumptions about God's nature and my dependence on Him. But in my supplication I am not calling attention to such assumptions. If I wanted to do so, I would say instead something like: "God is knowing, understanding, and discerning," or "I am dependent on God for knowledge, understanding, and discernment." And if I wanted to praise God for such qualities, I might say: "Praised art Thou who is knowing, understanding and discerning." But rather than doing any of these things, in making such a prayer as the fourth benediction of the Amidah I am simply making a request to God. Therefore if Petuchowski

---

14   St. Thomas Aquinas: Summa Theologica, vol. 39, p. 53.

means to argue that petitionary prayers are equivalent to prayers of praise because they contain presuppositions about God's nature and man's dependence on God, he is making a serious blunder by obscuring the intentions of the two types of prayers.

Another reductionist account of petitionary prayer is given by Louis Jacobs in Jewish Prayer. Here Jacobs asserts that in uttering a prayer of petition individuals acquire the proper attitude to their requests.[15] Furthermore, he writes, petitionary prayer "serves as a reminder of God's will."[16] Now it may be the case that when someone makes a request to God he acquires the proper attitude to the petition and is reminded of God's will. But this is not the main purpose of petitionary prayer. The point of praying to God in this way is to make a supplication, and Jacobs is mistaken if he believes that the difficulties connected with the notion of petitioning God can be removed by redefining the function of petitionary prayer along different lines. Thus it seems clear that Jacob's, Petuchowski's, as well as Phillips' reductionist accounts of the nature of supplicatory prayer are unsuccessful because they consciously omit the basic purpose of such petitions, namely asking God for something. The philosophical perplexities inherent in such an act must be faced directly without trying to portray petitionary prayers as something other than what they are.

---

15 L. Jacobs: Jewish Prayer, London, Jewish Chronicle Publications, p. 13.

16 Ibid. p. 14.

CHAPTER 4
MAKING REQUESTS TO GOD

The last chapter illustrated that any attempt to reduce petitionary prayers to expressions of praise or personal religious commitment is misguided. We must regard petitionary prayers as being genuine requests. But are petitionary prayers like the requests human beings make to one another? Or is there something characteristic about God's nature which makes talking to Him different from talking to humans? In The Concept of Prayer D.Z. Phillips poses this question as follows: "At first sight it may seem that talking to God is a mere instance of our talk to each other, the only difference being that the person addressed is not on earth, but lives in heaven.... The God to whom one prays is said to be a person.... If one calls God a person, does it follow that talking to Him is like talking to another person?"[1]

An atheist would answer this question by asserting that since God does not exist, praying to Him is really only a form of talking to oneself. According to this view petitionary prayer is merely an unsophisticated mode of self-suggestion and wishful thinking. But this argument confuses the issue. The point is not whether there is in fact a God who can listen and respond to petitionary prayers. The question is whether the believer himself when he prays thinks that there is someone "out there" whom he is addressing. Since petitionary prayer presupposes the existence of a divine reality distinct from the believer, it is impossible to interpret petitionary prayer as a type of internal communication. Indeed as Phillips remarks, "no matter how he explains it, it is essential for the believer to assert that he talks to someone other than himself when he prays. A

---

[1] D.Z. Phillips: The Concept of Prayer, pp. 41-43.

conviction that one is talking to oneself is the death of prayer."[2]

But if petitionary prayer is not a process of talking to oneself, how does talking to God compare with talking to others? At first sight, as Phillips writes,[3] it might appear that talking to God is no different from talking to human persons. Ancestor worship, he maintains, might seem to support such a view: "People talked to their fathers when they were alive, and continued to talk to them after they had died." But this view is misleading since it omits the fact that "bound up with ancestor worship is the belief in the special status of the dead. It is the status of the object addressed which determines the grammar of the talk: it is no longer people's daily discourse; it is worship of the dead."[4] Such worship presupposes that those who are worshipped are not able to respond verbally to what is said to them. "The will of the dead," Phillips writes, "is not like the will of the living... When one's parents are alive there is always the possibility of arguing with them, protesting against them, defying them, or reaching a compromise with them. No such possibility exists with the will of the dead."[5] From this analysis it appears that although there seems to be a parallel between speaking to God and speaking to individuals who have died, we should be cautious about stretching this analogy too far. Just as there are significant differences between speaking to one's parents when they are alive and worshipping them when they are dead, so too there are important distinctions between our talking to God and talking to each other.

---

2   Ibid. p. 14.

3   Ibid.

4   Ibid.

5   Ibid. p. 42.

According to Phillips, God is like one's ancestors who have died in that He does not respond verbally to requests made to Him. "The important point to note here," he writes, "is that God never says 'I am angry,' or anything else for that matter, in the way we do. This goes hand in hand with the fact that He is not seen, that is, is logically unseeable, in a state of anger. Normally, it is the prophet or the teacher who says that God is angry. Even when God's voice is said to say this from the midst of bushes or clouds, there is this necessary non-immediacy, as it were... God's ability to enter into relationships with me is not made possible by His being able to participate in a shared language...."[6]

How can one tell God anything? Phillip asks. "When we speak to other people, we often impart information," he states. "We tell them something, which otherwise they would not have known. But can we say this of our talk to God? Can we give Him information?"[7] If one believes that God knows everything, then it makes no sense to assume that it is possible to inform God of something He did not already know. But in Phillips' words "if God does not come to know anything, what is the believer doing when he talks to God?"[8] Phillips answers this question in a discussion concerning the confession of one's sins. "Although," he writes, "God does not come to know anything when one tells one's sins to Him, the person who confesses comes to know something about himself...."[9] Thus in Phillips' view when one makes a petitionary prayer, it is senseless to expect God to respond verbally to the request addressed to Him or to believe that one is informing Him about something He did

---

6 Ibid. pp. 47, 50.

7 Ibid. p. 53.

8 Ibid. p. 54.

9 Ibid. p. 56.

not already know. On the contrary, "God is told nothing, but in the telling, the person who confesses is told something about the state of his soul."[10]

Is this description of petitionary prayer consistent with the depiction of petitionary prayer found in the Bible? According to a literal interpretation of the Biblical text, Phillips' presentation is misguided. Throughout the Bible God frequently responds verbally to requests made to Him and at times appears to be ignorant of the information He receives. For example in the dialogue between Abraham and God,[11] God changes His mind concerning the decision to destroy Sodom. Here Abraham reminds God of the proper and just course of action that He had apparently forgotten: "Far be it from Thee to do this," he declared, "to kill good and bad together; for then the good would suffer with the bad.... Shall not the judge of all the earth do what is just?"[12] In response to this admonition, God said: "If I find in the city of Sodom fifty good men, I will pardon the whole place for their sake."[13] In addition God frequently appears to act on the basis of information conveyed to Him through prayer. For example after Amos pleaded with God to save Israel from her enemies, God repented because Amos reminded Him that Israel would be totally annihilated if her enemies were allowed to be victorious.[14] Such an anthropomorphic conception of God's nature and activity is a central feature of the Biblical narrative. He is often described

---

10   _Ibid_. p. 59.

11   Genesis 18:23-33.

12   Genesis 18:25.

13   Genesis 18:26.

14   Amos 7:2.

as possessing human attributes (a back side,[15] a palm,[16] a hand,[17] an outstretched arm,[18] a finger[19]); He is depicted as acting in the same way that humans do (He walks,[20] ascends,[21] returns,[22] comes,[23] sees,[24] hears,[25] smells,[26] knows[27]); and He also feels emotions (He grieves,[28] pities,[29] becomes angry[30]). God is also present at certain localities: in Ex. 33:9-11 He speaks to Moses in the tent of meeting; in Gen. 32:25-31 He appears to Jacob at Peniel; and in Gen. 3:8-13 He speaks to Adam and Eve in the Garden of Eden after having walked there.

A number of Biblical scholars have emphasized that such an anthropomorphic presentation of God may have initially been perceived as a true representation by the ancient Israelites-

---

[15]   Exodus 33:23.

[16]   Exodus 33:22.

[17]   Exodus 3:20.

[18]   Exodus 6:6.

[19]   Exodus 31:18.

[20]   Genesis 3:8.

[21]   Genesis 17:22.

[22]   Genesis 18:14.

[23]   Genesis 20:3.

[24]   Genesis 1:4.

[25]   Genesis 21:17.

[26]   Genesis 8:21.

[27]   Genesis 3:5.

[28]   Genesis 6:6.

[29]   Genesis 19:16.

[30]   Genesis 18:30.

only later did it come to have a figurative meaning. In the words of E. Bevan, "the old anthropomorphic language continued to be used as symbolic imagery long after the belief in its literal truth had disappeared... no doubt the process by which what was once understood literally came to be understood symbolically was a gradual one, with many confused intermediate stages in which the idea hovered between the literal and the symbolic.[31]   Again, W. Eichrodt writes: "It is true that a concrete conception of the panim (face) is also found in the popular tales of ancient Israel.   Thus, Jacob was astounded that he should have escaped with his life in spite of having seen the divine being with whom he had been wrestling, face to face, and he called the scene of his adventure Peniel (Face of God)."[32] On this view the expression "face of God" was used to mean originally that Jacob had actually seen God's face - it was only later that objections were raised to this naive view (according to Ex. 33:2 - "no one, not even such an elect man of God as Moses, can in any circumstances look upon the panim of God.")[33]

One reason for thinking the ancient Israelites initially conceived of God as possessing human-like attributes is that later Biblical editors appear to have substituted divine messengers for God in the text so that the impression would not be given that God appeared and spoke directly to human beings. For example in Genesis a messenger of God appeared to Hagar and proclaimed the destiny of her son despite the fact that after the angel vanished, Hagar stated that she had seen God

---

[31]   E. Bevan: <u>Symbolism and Belief</u>, pp. 44-45.

[32]   W. Eichrodt: <u>Old Testament Theology</u>, Vol. II, pp. 35-36.

[33]   <u>Ibid</u>.

Himself.[34]   This substitution of God's messenger for God Himself suggests that later writers did not want to give the impression that God looked and acted like a person; therefore they inserted a subordinate celestial being into the older Biblical account.   In line with this view some scholars argue that the fact that throughout the Bible, other expressions are used as substitutions for God's corporeal presence also indicates that later Biblical writers wanted to get away from the earlier notion that God appears in a human form.   For example in Ex. 24:16 the glory of God is described as a consuming fire resting on Mount Sinai. "It is precisely this priestly technical term of the kabod," W. Eichrodt writes, "which most clearly betrays the effort to play down any sensorily perceptible manifestation of God."[35]   In prophetic Judaism other forms of God's manifestation (such as the "name of God," "the spirit of God" and "the word of God") are also frequently substituted for God's corporeal presence. These substitutions were presumably used to give a different impression of the nature of God from that found in the older traditions.   Other scholars have offered different explanations to account for the prohibition against representing God anthropomorphically.   G. von Rad for example states: "[its] [the prohibition's] intention was not by any means to debar the people of Israel from representing God in concrete form." Rather, he writes, the intention of the prohibition was to emphasize the transcendence of God.[36]   Similarly M. Noth writes that the basis of the prohibition "lies in the idea, widespread in the ancient world, that an image had a firm connection with the being it portrayed, and that with the help of an image a man might gain power over the being represented in the image.

---

[34]   Genesis 16:13.

[35]   W. Eichrodt: Old Testament Theology, Vol. I, p. 408.

[36]   G. von Rad: Old Testament Theology, Edinburgh, Oliver & Boyd, 1962, Vol. I, pp. 218-219.

Israel is forbidden any image so that the people cannot even make the attempt to gain power over God or that which is of God."[37]

If the Biblical text was originally understood in such a literal fashion, God was conceived by the ancient Israelites as akin to a human person - a view opposite to that adopted by Phillips. When requests were made to Him, the ancient Israelites must have thought that He listened, was informed, and frequently responded verbally. Yet even on such an anthropomorphic view, God was not depicted exactly like a human person, and it is unlikely that the writers of the Bible conceived of God's features along the same lines as human physical characteristics. Indeed the fact that Scripture records that God appeared in natural phenomena (such as a thick cloud and fire) and depicts God as being able to appear and disappear illustrates the Biblical authors' conviction that God has a suprahuman nature. Given this qualified anthropomorphic understanding of God, how are we to interpret passages where God is depicted as appearing and speaking to individuals? In Exodus 33:9-11 we read: "When Moses entered it [the tent of meeting], the pillar of cloud came down, and stayed at the entrance to the tent and the Lord spoke with Moses.... The Lord would speak with Moses face to face, as one man speaks to another." On a literal reading of the text we should assume that the Biblical author must have believed that God was actually present in the tent and spoke to Moses directly. Presumably this implies that Moses saw God and heard Him speak - thus he was able to infer from this encounter what God was thinking and feeling. When we speak to others, we watch their physical responses - smiles, grimaces, frowns and so forth - to determine what they are communicating. Apparently the

---

[37]   M. Noth: Exodus, London, SCM Press, 1962, pp. 162-163.

ancient Israelites believed something like this occurred when Moses spoke with God face to face.

Here then we can see that Phillips' presentation of the mechanics of petitionary prayer is not supported by this early Biblical conception of God's activity. In making a request to God one would be speaking to Him in essentially the same way that one would speak to a person. One could assume that He would be informed about something which He might not otherwise know. For example in telling God of one's anguish and need, one could assume that God might not have an awareness of the severity of one's situation. Or one might anticipate (as Abraham seemed to do when he pleaded that Sodom be saved) that God is not fully aware of the kinds of actions He should perform. In both these cases one would speak to God as one might to a relative or friend, and it would not be inconceivable to think that God might reply. He might say yes or no.

Yet despite such similarities between speaking to God and to a human person, there are significant differences. One's reaction to God and the type of requests that could be posed to Him would be different in several respects from what occurs in human interactions. There would be no sense in commanding God to answer prayer. When we make requests to others, we sometimes formulate our demands in such terms. A father might command his son to do this or that. But when we petition God our requests do not have this force. We do not command God—rather we make supplications which we can only hope God will fulfil. Another difference between speaking to God and to humans is that unlike human beings, God in the Bible does not often respond. For example when Samson asked God for water to quench his thirst, God without speaking "cleaved the hollow place that is in Lehi, and there came water thereout." Of course human beings often simply do what is requested of them without saying anything. But in most cases we expect people to

respond to us unless it is impossible, unnecessary or
embarrassing for them to do so. And even if this does not take
place, there is almost invariably some indication whether the
person is going to comply. We rely on facial expressions, bodily
clues, and the like, or if the person is far away on a message
indicating what the individual intends to do. But when God is
asked for something, there is no reason to expect a verbal
response, nor should we expect God to appear before us. And if
our request goes unanswered, it would be misguided to expect an
explanation why. This is obviously radically different from the
expectations we have when we ask people for things. A final
difference between petitioning God and making requests to
others is that almost invariably we know the location of the
person to whom we are addressing. Knowing the location of the
person whom I speak to or the address of the person whom I
am writing to is a necessary condition for my request to be
fulfilled. But this is not the case with God.

So far we have been considering the process of praying to
God when He is conceived anthropomorphically (as in the
earliest traditions of the Bible). Here, as we have seen,
Phillips' analysis of petitionary prayer breaks down. But from
the time of the rabbis to the present day God was depicted as
incorporeal, omnipotent, all-good, omniscient, omnipresent, and
unchanging. Arguably this is the notion of God Phillips was
considering in his discussion of petitionary prayer. Given such
a theological conception, praying to God must be radically
different from making a request to a human person. If God
does not occupy space, it makes no sense to expect him to make
His presence manifest; if God has no body, it makes little sense
to expect a verbal response. Thus when Rabbi Eleazar, Rabbi
Johanan, Rabbi and Rab made personal petitions to God, in all
likelihood they did not expect God to appear to them in a
bodily state, to speak to them, or learn something He did not
already know. Similarly nowadays when a Jewish congregation

recites prayers of petition, they would be dumbfounded if God appeared in front of them, and they would jump out of their skins if a great voice boomed out in response to their prayers. A Jew does not expect God to answer him in the way he would expect his neighbour in the next seat to respond. Nor does he expect God to be informed by his petition as his neighbour would be.

To sum up, if God in fact corresponds to the earliest descriptions of Him in the Bible, then making a request to God is in many ways similar to making a request to another person. There would be no reason to assume that God could not be given new information by our prayers, or that He could not appear to us, reply verbally, or even explain the reasons for His decision to grant, or not to grant, our requests. But we should not expect Him to give a response or appear before us. However if God is totally unlike a human person as He has been depicted in rabbinic and later Judaism, making a request to Him is radically different from making a request to another person. There is no reason whatsoever to assume that He would respond verbally to our requests, and we would be wrong to think He might appear before us or be informed by our petitions.

CHAPTER 5
DIVINE INTERVENTIONS AND MIRACLES

In the last chapter we examined the various interpretations of what happens when we make requests to God; as we have seen, the intention of petitionary prayer remains the same regardless of which interpretation we accept: to ask God to intervene in our lives. When one asks God to answer such prayers, can one distinguish between the requests made to him? I mentioned in Chapter 2 that Jewish petitionary prayers fall roughly into three distinct groups, but it is also possible to divide Jewish petitionary prayers into two other categories: prayers for divine intervention and prayers for miracles. Now it might seem that if one prays for a particular thing to happen and God grants the request, such a divine intervention would by definition be a miracle. In Essays in the Philosophy of Religion, H.H. Price argues that divine interventions made in response to petitionary prayer are "minor miracles." "Suppose," he writes "that you have promised to visit a friend in a town you have never been to before, and you get lost. It is Sunday evening and pouring with rain. There is no one about in the streets. You have no map of the town, or if you have, you forgot to bring it with you. All you know is that your friend's address is No. 15 Acacia Street. Then, if you are a very pious person, you may ask for God's help. 'Please, Lord, may I find Tom's house'.... And then a few minutes later you see someone opening his front door to let the cat out. You ask him where Acacia Street is. He tells you to take the first turning on the right, and then the third turning on the left, and you get to your friend's house no more than ten minutes later."[1]

Was it just a coincidence that the man happened to let the cat out at that particular time? Price asks. Of course it might have been. But if it were not a coincidence, then what could

---

[1]   H.H. Price: Essays in the Philosophy of Religion, Oxford, Clarendon Press, 1972, pp. 44-45.

the explanation be? "Are we to say that when you received what you asked for," Price continues, "this came about by a kind of ad hoc divine intervention, whereby the man was 'made' to walk at such a speed that you would reach the spot just when the cat was being let out? This might be described as the 'miraculous' theory of the way petitionary prayers are answered. It would amount to saying that God works a kind of minor miracle on the praying person's behalf."[2]

According to Price's view petitionary prayers which are efficacious are instances of "minor miracles." But what exactly does he mean by the term? "A miracle," he writes "is by definition something exceptional, 'extraordinary' in the literal sense of the word; and this is still true if the miracle is, so to speak, a very little one."[3] Thus Price believes that divine interventions - like the case of a man finding his friend's house - were "very little" extraordinary events and thereby miraculous. Is this definition accurate? On the basis of the widest definition of miracles as "extraordinary events" Price would be correct. Whatever one might mean by "extraordinary events," there would be no question that divine interventions would belong to this category. But on a narrower definition of miracle there are difficulties with Price's presentation. Since the seventeenth century we have come to think of the behaviour of things as governed by laws of nature which prescribe what events must follow other events. Such natural laws may be universal or statistical. Universal laws state what must happen; statistical laws state what must probably happen in a particular case. Paradigm examples of universal laws are Newton's three laws of motion and his law of gravitation whereas paradigms of statistical laws are the laws governing the behaviour of photons and electrons. On the basis of this understanding of the

---

2   Ibid. p. 45.

3   Ibid.

physical universe, it is frequently asserted by philosophers of religion and theologians that events which would go against natural laws are miracles. According to this definition, the notion of an "extraordinary event" is defined in terms of a violation of the laws of nature. This was the definition given by Hume in an Enquiry Concerning Human Understanding. "A miracle," he wrote, "may be accurately defined [as] a transgression of a law of nature by a particular volition of the Deity."[4] On the basis of this interpretation Price would be wrong in thinking that all divine interventions are "minor miracles." On the contrary, only those divine interventions which violate the laws of nature would be considered miraculous. For example when Price argues that the man was "made" to let his cat out, or when the visitor was "made" to walk at such and such a speed, there would be no reason to think that such divine interventions were cases of miracles. There are no violations of any natural laws involved in such instances - these were merely ordinary events.

Let us then turn to Divine interventions made in response to prayer which do not violate any laws of nature (and are on this definition not strictly speaking miraculous). As we have seen, petitionary prayers can roughly be divided into three types: (1) prayers for tangible objects such as Jacob's prayer for food and clothing, Samson's prayer for something to drink, and Hannah's prayer for a son; (2) requests for God to bring about a change in an individual's or a collective group's psychological, physical, intellectual or religious attitude and welfare (such as the psalmist's plea for God to be gracious to Israel and heal her); and (3) prayers for God to bring about an event such as Abraham's plea to save Sodom, and Joshua's prayer for God's help in defeating the Amorites. The presupposition of such

---

[4] D. Hume: "Enquiry Concerning Human Understanding." In The English Philosophers from Bacon to Mill, New York, The Modern Library, 1939, p. 115.

prayers is that God can grant these requests. In the Bible God is described as stating that He will answer prayers addressed to Him. For example when Amos pleaded with God to forgive Israel, God decreed that He would spare her. When Samson asked God for something to drink, God cleaved a hollow place out of which flowed water. In such cases as these God presumably did not need to violate the laws of nature: He merely acted in conformity with nature. Again when Hannah asked God to send her a son there is no reason to think that God was compelled to bring about a miracle - He could have simply acted as an agent in bringing about an event in accordance with the process of conception and childbirth. The same is the case with Samson's request for water. In this situation God could have acted entirely in accordance with the laws which govern physical objects. And there is no reason to suppose that in order to hew out the hollow place at Lehi, He needed to suspend the law of gravity or the law of the conservation of energy. In other words, when God is described as granting requests in response to petitionary prayers, we can assume that a supernatural agent (in addition to the ordinary causal agents which operate in our everyday life) was at work in the world.

Yet there are serious difficulties in understanding how God could have fulfilled requests even when He is conceived anthropomorphically. In the case of prayers for tangible objects, we could have some idea what it would be like for God to grant simple requests but what was God's activity in causing Hannah to conceive? How are we to imagine God causing fire to descend from Heaven so as to ignite the sacrifice in the presence of the followers of Baal and the ancient Israelites? These difficulties increase when we consider the third type of petitionary prayers - requests for God to bring about events. There are some events where it is quite simple to imagine God's agency if He is conceived as an identifiable person. For example if we believe that God can stop evil from occurring (as Rabbi did when he asked God to cause him to be delivered from evil happenings), it is possible to imagine God acting like a divine policeman. But what would it be like for God to destroy an entire city? Or how could God cause Israel to be full of disciples? Again how could God help in defeating the Amorites as Joshua requested? This problem is greatest when we consider the second type of petitionary prayers: prayers for God to bring about a change in an individual's or collective group's psychological, physical, intellectual, or religious attitude. If God is conceived as an identifiable person, we could imagine God privately encouraging and inspiring individuals so that they would be strengthened and comforted (in the way humans converse with one another). But if this is not what God does in response to prayer, what is the nature of His activity? We can see then that although in certain situations it is possible to imagine how God can fulfill requests if He is understood anthropomorphically, there are other cases which are particularly problematic.

When we conceive of God as totally unlike a human person, our difficulties increase. Here it would be impossible to have any clear evidence of God answering prayer. Suppose for example that we ask God to cure a person who has become very ill. If we believe that God is essentially like an identifiable person, we could hope He would appear visibly and cure him. If he did, he would act in much the same fashion as a doctor or a nurse. And just as we have evidence that an ill person is cured because he was operated on by a surgeon, so we might be able to have evidence that the ill person was cured by God. If we were questioned whether God was the agent in restoring his health we could reply: "There is no question. God appeared and cured the person. We saw Him." But, if we believe that God is not at all like a human person, then we would not be able to respond in this way - there would be no way of ascertaining whether God was the cause of the cure; we would lack any evidence to offer in support of the contention that God was the agent in restoring the individual's health.

I mentioned at the beginning of this chapter that divine interventions can be grouped into two categories: those which do not violate the laws of nature and those which do. So far we have looked at those divine interventions which are constant with the laws of nature. But what are we to say about divine interventions which violate natural laws? Do they raise special problems? Most of the petitionary prayers contained in the Bible, Rabbinic literature, and the Jewish Prayer Book are supplications for God to intervene without violating the laws of nature, yet there are notable exceptions. We read in Joshua 8:12-15, for example, that "On the day when the Lord delivered the Amorites into the hands of Israel, Joshua spoke with the Lord, and he said in the presence of Israel: 'Stand still, O Sun, in Gibeon; stand, Moon, in the Vale of Aijalon'."[5] Here Joshua prayed that God would allow the sun and moon to remain fixed in the sky so that Israel could defeat the Amorites. In response to Joshua's request, "the sun stood still and the moon halted until a nation had taken vengeance on its enemies.... The sun stayed in the mid heaven and made no haste to set for almost a whole day. Never before or since has there been such a day as this day on which the Lord listened to the voice of man."[6] In Exodus 4:4-9 we also have several examples of miraculous divine interventions made in response to prayer. Afraid that Israel would not believe or listen to him, Moses asked God for some means by which he could demonstrate to Israel that he was a true prophet. In reply, "God said, 'What have you there in your hand?' 'A staff,' Moses answered. The Lord said, 'Throw it on the ground.' Moses threw it down and it turned into a snake.

---

[5]   Joshua 8:12.

[6]   Joshua 8:13-14.

He ran away from it, but the Lord said, 'Put your hand out and seize it by the tail.' He did so and gripped it firmly, and it turned back into a staff in his hand."[7] "Then, the Lord said, 'Put your hand inside the fold of your cloak.' He did so, and when he drew it out the skin was diseased, white as snow. The Lord said, 'Put it back again', and he did so. When he drew it out this time it was as healthy as the rest of his body."[8] The miraculous character of these events made them particularly convincing evidence that Moses was truly speaking in God's name. In this regard God stated, "If they do not believe you and do not accept the evidence of the first sign, they may accept the evidence of the second. But if they are not convinced even by these two signs, and will not accept what you say, then fetch some water from the Nile and pour it out on the dry ground, and the water you take from the Nile will turn to blood on the ground."[9]

These four Biblical examples of miraculous divine interventions are unusual in several respects. Most Jews today would not ask God to perform similar extraordinary actions. But sometimes when Jews ask God to heal the sick, they are in effect asking God to suspend the laws of nature. A believer for example who had a relative suffering from terminal cancer would no doubt be thinking of him when he prayed the seventh benediction of the Amidah ("Heal us, O Lord, and we shall be healed...."). Here he would be asking God to heal his relative by intervening in the laws of nature in order to cause the natural growth of the cancer to stop or disappear altogether. Again Jewish parents whose child's arms had been severed from his body in an automobile accident, might pray in desperation: "O God, please restore his arms. Make them as they were

---

7   Exodus 4:2-4.

8   Exodus 4:6-7.

9   Exodus 4:8-9.

before." How can we know whether such prayers could ever be efficacious? In considering such divine interventions, we are confronted with the same problems met in considering divine interventions consonant with the laws of nature. But in the cases of miraculous divine interventions, we are faced with other difficulties. If I ask God to send rain and it does rain, then what I requested occurred. There would of course be a question whether it rained because I asked God to make it rain, but no one would dispute that what was being requested took place. But with regard to alleged miracles, there is the question whether such divine interventions actually happened. How are we to determine whether miraculous events which are claimed to be answers to petitionary prayers have actually taken place?

In _An Enquiry Concerning Human Understanding_, Hume considered the issue of miracles and claimed that when one conducts an enquiry concerning whether a miracle has taken place, one must proceed as anyone conducting any enquiry (and in particular any historical enquiry). One must, "proportion his belief to the evidence."[10] Since the evidence against the occurrence of any purported miracle is extremely strong and must outweigh the evidence in favour of the occurrence, we may reasonably conclude that no miraculous event ever happened. In support Hume argued that "there is not to be found, in all history, any miracle attested by a sufficient number of men, of such unquestioned good sense, education and learning as to secure us against all delusions in themselves."[11] Further, a religious enthusiast may make up miraculous stories, which he knows to be false in order to propagate his faith. "A religionist," Hume writes, "may be an enthusiast... [and] may know his narrative to be false, and yet persevere in it, with the

---

10   D. Hume: _Enquiry Concerning Human Understanding_, p. 110.

11   _Ibid_. p. 116.

best intentions in the world, for the sake of promoting so holy a cause."[12] Hume also argued that "it forms a strong presumption against all supernatural and miraculous relations, that they are observed chiefly to abound among ignorant and barbarous nations."[13] Finally, since each religious tradition claims validity on the grounds of its own alleged miracles, we find that each set of miraculous events contradicts every other set. It is impossible "that the religions of ancient Rome, of Turkey, of Siam and of China should, all of them, be established on any solid foundation. Every miracle, therefore, pretended to have been wrought in any of these religions (and all of them abound in miracles), as its direct scope is to establish the particular system to which it is attributed; so has it the same force, though more indirectly, to overthrow every other system. In destroying a rival system, it likewise destroys the credit of those miracles, on which that system was established."[14]

Since the seventeenth century we have come to think of the behaviour of things as governed by the laws of nature. According to traditional physics, the physical world is often conceived as moving in space and time. Every motion is believed to have a cause. No change could take place in this system unless it were previously determined. As it is impossible for a billiard ball to move without being hit by another billiard ball, so there could be no uncaused event in the physical universe. The laws governing the physical world are universal and cannot be violated. On this view violations of such universally valid laws are simply impossible. Yet as R. Swinburne points out, "since the development of Quantum Theory in this century many scientists have come to hold that the fundamental natural laws are statistical. These are the laws

---

12   Ibid. p. 117.

13   Ibid. p. 119.

14   Ibid. p. 121.

governing the behaviour of the fundamental particles, such as photons, electrons, and mesons, out of which the ordinary familiar objects which surround us are composed."[15]   As Swinburne notes, if the laws of the universe are universal, they could not be violated.   But if the basic laws of the universe are statistical, although it would be highly improbable that there would be an exception to such statistical laws, it is not inconceivable.   "If the laws of nature are statistical," Swinburne writes, "and not universal as Quantum Theory suggests, it is not in all cases so clear what counts as a counter-instance to them. A universal law is a law of the form 'all so-and-sos do such-and-such' and a counter-instance is therefore a so-and-so which does not do such-and-such.   The occurrence of such a counter-instance is an occurrence of an exception to the law." Swinburne continues this explanation of an exception to a statistical law by using an example from thermodynamics.   "It is formally compatible with the currently accepted statistical version of the second law of thermodynamics," he writes, "that a kettle of water put on a fire freeze instead of boiling.   But it is vastly improbable that such an event will ever happen within human experience.   Hence if it does happen, it is not unnaturally described as an exception to the law."[16]   Thus according to this view, it is no longer viewed as impossible that events, such as a kettle of water freezing on a fire, could take place.   It is only highly unlikely, and this contemporary understanding of the laws of nature (in contrast to the classical picture of the physical universe), demonstrates that miracles could in fact occur, though their occurrence would be vastly improbable.

If it is no longer feasible to claim that violations of the laws of nature are impossible, does the balance of evidence

---

15   R. Swinburne: <u>The Concept of Miracle</u>, pp. 18-21.

16   <u>Ibid</u>. p. 3.

suggest that miracles have not occurred? Hume supported this assertion by arguing that no miracle has been attested by a sufficient number of men. But what would count as an adequate number? Nowhere does Hume answer this question. Indeed he seemed to imply that no number of men could be sufficient. Discussing the miracles allegedly to have occurred at the Tomb of Abbé Paris, Hume wrote, "Many of the miracles were immediately proved upon the spot, before judges of unquestioned integrity, attested by witnesses of credit and distinction.... And what have we to oppose to such a cloud of witnesses, but the absolute impossibility or miraculous nature of the events, which they relate? And this surely, in the eyes of all reasonable people, will alone be regarded as a sufficient refutation."[17] In other words, Hume suggested that there could never be a sufficient number of witnesses to demonstrate that a miracle took place. As Swinburne writes, "Here the credibility of the witnesses in terms of their number, integrity and education is dismissed, not as inadequate, but as irrelevant."[18] Thus, it appears that when Hume wrote that there has not been found in "all history, any miracle attested by a sufficient number of men, of such unquestioned good sense, education, and learning...", he judged these witnesses by whether they accepted miracles or not. If they did, then by definition they could not be regarded as men of good repute.

If Hume's account is biased, how are we to judge whether alleged miracles have in fact occurred? What are the types of evidence that should be considered, and what are the standards we should use for judging this information? Hume, in his discussion, concentrated primarily on the testimony of witnesses, but as Swinburne points out there are other types of evidence

---

[17] D. Hume: Enquiry Concerning Human Understanding, p. 124.

[18] R. Swinburne: The Concept of Miracle, p. 16.

as well.   There are, he writes, "four kinds of evidence about what happened at some past instant - our own apparent memories of our past experiences, the testimony of others about their past experiences, physical traces and our contemporary understanding of what things are physically impossible or improbable."[19]   One way of weighing evidence, Swinburne suggests, is to obtain as coherent a picture as possible of the past as consistent as possible with the evidence.   This idea, he believes, could be formulated into a single rule: "Accept as many pieces of evidence as possible."[20]   Although this is good advice, it certainly is not sufficient for determining what evidence is acceptable.

To summarize, we have seen in this chapter that when God is understood anthropomorphically and viewed as manifesting Himself in response to prayer and bringing about a non-miraculous divine intervention, there are a number of problems about such activity.   In some cases such as when God is requested to grant a tangible object, it is possible to have some idea how God could fulfil such a request.   But when it comes to understanding how God could grant a child, ignite a burnt-offering, destroy a city or impart comfort, this is much more difficult to conceive.   And when God is described as bringing about miraculous divine interventions in response to prayer, we are not only faced by the same perplexities as with non-miraculous interventions, but we also cannot even be certain whether the alleged miracles actually took place.   When we conceive of God in a non-anthropomorphic way, these difficulties become even more serious.   We could have no evidence that He had heard or granted our requests, and even if He did intervene, we would have no means of knowing whether it was really Him.

---

19   _Ibid_. p. 33.

20   _Ibid_., p. 37.

CHAPTER 6

THE EFFICACY OF PETITIONARY PRAYERS

Throughout Jewish history Jews have believed that God answers their prayers. In the Bible for example after Hannah prayed to God for a son, she conceived a child. The text states explicitly that God caused Hannah to conceive and she herself recognized this fact by calling her son Samuel because, as she said, "I have asked him of the Lord."[1] Similarly when fire descended from the sky and kindled the burnt-offering in front of the Ancient Israelites, Elijah and the Israelites believed that God was the cause. It is for this reason that when people saw the fire, "they fell prostrate and cried, 'The Lord is God, the Lord is God'."[2] In Rabbinic literature as well it is affirmed that God answers prayers. This was so despite the fact that, as A. Marmorstein points out, "the efficacy of prayers was often, seriously and lightly, argued about.... Here the question may have been how can God hear all the prayers uttered at different places at the same time? How can God fulfil the contradictory requests of the various worshippers in the same place? One wants rain, the other drought?.... If God's decrees are settled, how can prayer upset them?" Yet despite these difficulties it was, as Marmorstein notes, "a well-established doctrine of Rabbinic theology that prayer can bring about changes and is effective."[3]

According to the rabbis, prayer was a means by which death, famine, plague, drought, flood, earthquake, war, storm and other evils could be averted from the individual as well as from the community. As Marmorstein remarks, "instances of this generally-held view can be brought from history as well as

---

[1]   I Samuel 1:20.

[2]   I Kings 18:39.

[3]   A. Mormorstein: <u>The Old Rabbinic Doctrine of God</u>, London, Oxford University Press, 1927, p. 166.

legends, homilies, and teachings."[4]   In this regard for example R. Jose b. Halafta wrote "There are appointed times for prayer. Which time is the most favorable?   When the community deliver their prayers.   Therefore must man rise early for prayers, for there is nothing greater than prayer.   Do know, it was decreed concerning Moses that he should not enter the land, and not see it.   Thanks to his prayers, God has shown him the land. Hezekiah prayed, and the decree was annulled.   So Jacob, in sending his sons to Egypt prayed on their behalf."[5]   Similarly, R. Eleazar stated, "Dost thou want to know the strength of prayer?   If it does not accomplish the whole of it (the request), it does half of it."[6]   In the Talmud it is recorded that R. Hanina b. Dosa was celebrated for effecting cures by his prayer. He could tell whether his efforts would prove successful and he would say, "This patient will live" or "This patient will die." This he could determine by whether the prayer flowed freely from his mouth.   If it did, then his prayer would be granted; if it did not, then his prayer would not be granted.   Indeed R. Hanina's prayers were reputed to be so efficacious that R. Johanan b. Zakkai relied more on R. Hanina than on himself when prayers were needed for his sick child.   "Although I am greater in learning than Hanina," R. Johanan b. Zakkai stated, "he is more efficacious in prayer.   I am, indeed, the prince, but he is the steward who has constant access to the king." According to other Rabbinic authorities, "God hears all the prayers which are delivered at the same time.   God's ears hear all the supplications and entreaties addressed to him!"[7]   In another homily it is asserted that although God does not have

---

4   Ibid. p. 167.

5   Ibid.

6   Ibid. (see also Deuteronomy R. 8:1).

7   Ibid. (see also Exodus R. 21:4).

the sense organs which idols allegedly possess, He is nevertheless able to hear prayer. We read in this regard: "Idols have eyes, ears, nostrils, hands, legs, and cannot use them. God, however, has none of these things; yet He sees everything at the same time. He hears the prayers of all."[8]

Moreover it was a general principle in Rabbinic teaching that God's decrees are subject to change. R. Johanan for example taught in the name of R. Jose b. Halafta: "No word which went out from the mouth of God for good, even conditionally, was withdrawn. Only those which are for the good of the world, not so the decrees for evil and punishment, which are subject to alteration."[9] Similarly, it was maintained in popular belief that a Zaddik could annul the decrees of God.[10] Of course in many cases where petitionary prayers were offered to God, the requests were not fulfilled and this constituted a serious problem for the rabbis. If the requests were reasonable and if God had the power to grant them, there was every reason to think these requests would be granted. But since they were not, one could conclude that petitionary prayers are not in fact efficacious - this however was a view which the rabbis consistently resisted. Even when confronted by the criticisms of non-Jews, they affirmed their faith in God's power to respond to petitionary prayer. For example in a Rabbinic legend it was reported that a Roman (Tineius Rufus) said to the martyrs of Lydda, Julianus and Pappus before they were about to be executed, "He [God] cannot save you, as He saved the three young men, because He grew old since then, as it is said: 'The Lord does not see, and the God of Jacob does not

---

8   Ibid.

9   Ibid. p. 170 (see also Ber. 7a).

10   Ibid.

understand.'."[11]   In response to this taunt the martyrs defended
God.   "They [the three young men] were pious," they said, "and
the kind also worthy that a miracle should be performed through
them.   Thou, however, art unworthy, and we also are not
without guilt.   There are many wild beasts that could or should
put us to death at God's command.   Thou art one of them!"[12]
Here Julianus and Pappus asserted that God had the power to
save them, but it was their unworthiness which prevented Him
from doing so.   Therefore, they implied, the fact that they were
going to be executed did not show that God is incapable of
responding to prayer.

Even in the face of the most agonizing difficulties and
sufferings, the rabbis asserted that God has the power to
respond to prayer.   R. Simai for example used a parable
concerning the sun to refute the claim that God's power is
limited.   "Have you ever heard that the sun is sick, and is
unable to discharge his duties?" he asked.   "That the moon is
sick and unable to do her work?   God's servants are free from
weakness; can God Himself be sick?"   Similarly Bar Kappara
taught that God could make the impossible possible, the invisible
visible."[13]   From these examples we can see that although the
rabbis were aware of the difficulties raised by the fact that not
all petitionary prayers are answered, they nevertheless affirmed
that this was no obstacle in believing that God can and does
fulfil the requests made to Him.   The Prayer Book also
presupposes that God answers prayer.   In this regard L. Jacobs
writes, "The Hebrew Prayer Book contains many petitions, most
of them on behalf of the community rather than the individual
worshipper, yet all assuming that God answers the prayers of

---

[11]   Psalm 94.7.

[12]   A. Marmorstein: The Old Rabbinic Doctrine of God, p.
172.

[13]   Ibid. p. 173.

those who pray to Him."[14] From this survey, we can see that in the Bible, Rabbinic sources, and the Jewish Prayer Book, Jews asserted their conviction that God can and does answer prayers.

What is the nature of this process of responding to prayer? In our daily life we use the word "answer" in a variety of ways: when we are asked questions, we designate our replies as "answers"; we say that our question has been answered rightly or wrongly when we receive a reply relevant to our inquiry. We also use the word "answer" in relation to salutations. The word "answer" can in addition refer to the response to a letter, or indeed, as anything which is said, written, or done as a reply. Further the word "answer" can be used to designate that a person is responsible for a certain state of affairs. We might say for example, "This person is answerable for that action." And we also use the word "answer" to indicate that something has met a particular need. But in the case of prayer the word "answer" serves quite a different function. When we say: "God answered my request" we do not mean that God gave a verbal response to a question, nor that He acknowledged some sort of greeting. We mean that a request was granted. This is Price's understanding of the meaning of the word "answer" in relation to prayer: "Are we to say that when you received what you asked for, this came about by a kind of ad hoc divine intervention....? This might be described as the 'miraculous' theory of the way petitionary prayers are answered."[15]

Although this understanding of the function of the word "answer" in the context of prayer is generally assumed, we should note that it is possible and certainly acceptable to say that God answered a petitionary prayer even if the request was denied. This is the point Jacobs has in mind when he tells the story of a little girl who prayed repeatedly for a bicycle,

---

14   L. Jacobs: Jewish Prayer, p. 8.

15   H.H. Price: Essays in the Philosophy of Religion, p. 45.

without success: "You see," taunted her unbelieving friend, "God does not answer prayer." "Oh yes He does," answered the girl, "His answer was No!"[16] This conception of the notion of "answering prayers" is based on the ordinary understanding of what happens when requests are made - we know the answer may be either yes or no. We would consider a negative response to our request just as much an answer as a positive response. Thus Jacobs maintains that when our petitions to God are not granted, this does not mean that God has refused to answer our prayers; it only means that His answer was "no." This conception of petitionary prayers presupposes that all petitionary prayers are answered by God. On this view when one prays for something and what is prayed for takes place, God has in most cases answered "yes" to the requests addressed to Him. Similarly in those cases where one prays for something and what is prayed for does not occur, God has answered "no." God thus always gives an answer to prayer: either yes or no. It would be impossible in principle to point to a counter-example. According to this understanding of petitionary prayer, it is impossible to demonstrate that God does not answer prayers— the thesis that God answers all prayers is unassailable. But does this view accurately describe what happens when we pray to God? Certainly this contention is different from a scientific theory; it does not predict future events, nor does it describe how God makes or fulfils His decrees. Nevertheless this view does resemble a scientific theory in that it attempts to explain a particular phenomenon: what is entailed in answering petitionary prayers. This thesis makes a universal assertion: "God answers all prayers." But how are we to evaluate such a claim? According to Karl Popper, the test for determining whether a theory is acceptable in principle is whether it is open to refutation. "A scientist," he writes, "whether theorist or

---

16   L. Jacobs: _Jewish Prayer_, p. 16.

experimenter, puts forward statements, or systems of statements, and tests them step by step. In the field of the empirical sciences, more particularly, he constructs hypotheses, or systems of theories, and tests them against experience by observation and experiment.[17] The person who formulates a theory, Popper writes, must be interested in observation and testing, because, he argues, this is the only means by which he can determine whether his theory is corroborated by experience. "I shall," he argues, "admit a system as empirical or scientific only if it is capable of being tested by experience... it must be possible for an empirical scientific system to be refuted by experience."[18] Since the proposition that God answers all prayers is in principle irrefutable because there is no way to cite a counter-example, it cannot be tested in this way. Thus, in Popper's view, such a thesis is unacceptable because it cannot be corroborated by experience.

Let us now turn to a consideration of the belief that God answers "yes" to some requests and grants them. The belief that God has granted some petitionary prayers (or that petitionary prayers are sometimes efficacious), is, as T.R. Miles notes, composed of two assumptions. The first is that "prayers sometimes produce results"; the second is that "these results are caused by God." Obviously, as Miles points out, "If God answers prayer (in the sense that He grants the requests made to Him), both these assertions must be true also."[19] Despite the fact that the statement "God answers all prayers" is not open to testing, the assertion "prayers sometimes produce results" is, according to Miles, a testable claim. There is no short cut, he

---

[17] K. Popper: The Logic of Scientific Discovery, London, Hutchinson & Co., 1972, p. 27.

[18] Ibid. p. 41.

[19] T.R. Miles: Religion and the Scientific Outlook, London, George Allen & Unwin Ltd., 1959, p. 181.

writes, "to determining its truth or falsity; the only possible procedure is to examine all available evidence."[20] Such an assertion, he argues, could be made only on the basis of observation and experiment. "And this being so," Miles remarks, "there is no objection in principle to that characteristic empirical device, a controlled experiment with statistics. An example of such an experiment would be a comparison of the recovery rate in a wing of a hospital where ordinary methods of treatment are used with the recovery rate in another wing where these methods were supplemented by prayer."[21] According to Miles, such a test needs to be referred not to the individual conscience but to the appropriate scientific investigator.[22]

Miles is correct that the statement "prayers sometimes produce results" could in principle be verified statistically. If prayer makes a difference to the world, this should be able to be proved in the way that Miles outlines. However in all likelihood most believers would feel that such a controlled experiment is the wrong way to approach the problem. The devout do not accept that prayers sometimes produce results on the basis of a scientifically conducted experiment; rather they claim the efficacy of prayer on the basis of their own religious experience. For example an individual who had been in a plane which had serious engine trouble might well believe that the plane did not crash because of the prayer he made. He would not arrive at this conclusion because he had done a statistical investigation of what the other passengers did when they learnt the plane was in trouble. Rather he would adopt this view on the basis of his own personal situation. Similarly a believer would not be swayed by an adverse statistical analysis. If

---

20   Ibid.

21   Ibid. p. 182.

22   Ibid.

controlled experiments were done in a hospital comparing the rate of recovery of patients who were prayed for as against those who were not, and it was shown that patients who were prayed for recovered at exactly the same rate as those who were not prayed for, this would not shake his belief. Thus though the assertion "prayers sometimes produce results" could be based on observed facts, in practice this claim is accepted through the believer's existential experience and would not be abandoned even if a controlled experiment demonstrated that prayer makes no observable difference. The same point applies to the second assumption contained in the claim that God grants some petitionary prayers: "these results come from God." A religious person only says that results are caused by God if he presupposes that God frequently does produce them. If an individual believed that God had saved him from dying in a road accident, his belief would not be affected by any study of drivers' responses to motor accidents or any other counter-evidence of this type. Thus the belief in the efficacy of prayer seems to be based on two propositions, neither of which would be rejected by the believer because of a statistical experiment. Believers in prayer want to say that the proposition "petitionary prayers are sometimes efficacious" is a fact, but it is difficult to see how such a claim could be factual. "The world is round" is a fact - if one is an astronaut, one can see that for oneself; "the moon is made of green cheese" is a mistake - if one lands on the moon, one can taste for oneself that this is not the case. But the idea that prayers are sometimes answered is of a different order.

Allowing that believers regard the proposition "God answers some prayers" as a factual one, we must see if there is any way to refute it. Anthony Flew contends that all beliefs about God cannot be falsified. In <u>New Essays in Philosophical Theology,</u> he writes

"... it often seems to people who are not religious as if there was no conceivable event or series of events the occurrence of which would be admitted by sophisticated religious people to be a sufficient reason for conceding 'There wasn't a God after all' or 'God does not really love us then'. Someone tells us that God loves us as a father loves his children. We are reassured. But then we see a child is dying of inoperable cancer of the throat. His earthly father is driven frantic in his efforts to help, but his Heavenly Father reveals no obvious sign of concern.

Some qualification is made - God's love is 'not merely human love' or it is 'an inscrutable love,' perhaps- and we realise that such suffering are [sic] quite compatible with the truth of the assertion that 'God loves us as a father'.... We are reassured again. But then perhaps we ask: what is this assurance of God's (appropriately qualified) love worth, what is this apparent guarantee really a guarantee against? Just what would have to happen not merely (morally and wrongly) to tempt but also (logically and rightly) to entitle us to say 'God does not love us' or even 'God does not exist'?"[23]

Flew's analysis of theological statements also applies to petitionary prayers. If I say, "My petitionary prayer to God was efficacious - it produced what I requested from God," is there any situation which would force me to admit that I was mistaken? It seems there is not. As we have seen, no statistical survey would be sufficient to convince a believer that his prayers are not in fact efficacious. Likewise he would not be swayed by specific examples of prayers which were not effective. For example a person who believed in the efficacy of

_____

[23] A. Flew and A. MacIntyre (Eds.): <u>New Essays in Philosophical Theology</u>, London, SCM Press, 1955, pp. 96-99.

petitionary prayer might be told the following story by a bereaved father who had just lost his family in a fire: "My wife and I were asleep in bed when we were awakened by the cries of our children in the room next to ours. When we awoke, we saw flames around us. My wife screamed, and I was totally bewildered. There was a cloud of smoke in the room and fire everywhere. My wife clung to me, and I prayed, 'Oh God, let us survive. Please God, save the children!' Suddenly, I heard the sound of fire engines and I knew help had come. But I was terrified about what might have happened to the children. Somehow I made my way through our blazing room to the door, and I saw my two sons dead on the floor of the hall. They had burned to death as they tried to escape. When I saw them, I fainted. This is all I remember. But in the hospital, they told me that my wife had died too. The firemen did not rescue her in time even though they managed to save me."

Would such a tragic story as this change the mind of someone who believes in the efficacy of prayer? If God is all good ánd omnipotent, there would seem to be no reason why God would not have granted the poor person's prayer. The individual who believes in the efficacy of prayer might be moved by this story and possibly perplexed by its implications, but he would in all likelihood refuse to abandon his belief that God grants petitions. He would make some qualification to his original view. He might say "God does grant petitionary prayer, but God's will is inscrutable and therefore we should not expect all petitionary prayers to be granted." If he were questioned about this particular case, he would probably make a further qualification. He might say: "Ah, yes, this does seem like a case where God did not act justly. But God's justice is not merely human justice, and therefore we cannot judge God on the basis of our own human moral concepts." In other words, regardless of the number of examples of petitionary prayers which were not granted, the person who believes in the efficacy of prayer would not waver from his conviction.

It might be objected that this is an oversimplification. One could argue that it is possible to account for some of the cases where God did not grant the petitions which were addressed to Him. H.D. Lewis writes: "Not every prayer is for a sufficiently worthy end. Men do indeed sometimes pray for ends which it is preposterous to expect God to bless in any way. If I pray for terrible destruction to fall on my enemy or request that fire from heaven should consume those who oppose me, then I am seeking God's cooperation in matters not consistent with His character and declared purpose." Thus, he continues, "a vast number of unanswered prayers will fall into the class of prayers for radically unworthy ends which it is wrong, indeed blasphemous and not merely ill-judged to make the subject of prayer."[24] Lewis however is mistaken in thinking that he can dismiss the problem of unanswered prayers in this way. The case I just cited was a worthy prayer; there seems to be no reason why it should not have been granted.

To sum up, we can see that the principle that "God answers all prayers" is unassailable. There is no evidence either in favour of it or against it. But there are important differences between this claim and the claim that "petitionary prayers are sometimes efficacious." In this chapter we have seen that though people do not make this claim on the basis of scientific tests, they usually believe in the efficacy of petitionary prayer on the basis of some personal experience. Moreover in order for the claim that "petitionary prayers are sometimes efficacious" to be true, we need at least one instance of a prayer to God being followed by the occurrence of what was requested. This marginal experiential basis would not constitute a sufficient condition for the claim to be true; rather

---

24   H.D. Lewis: <u>Our Experience of God</u>, pp. 258-259.

it should be regarded as a necessary condition. Finally there might be some cases (though they would be notable exceptions) where the believer in the efficacy of prayer would base his claim on the evidence of God's manifestation in response to his prayer. Yet despite these minimal evidential bases, it seems impossible to convince someone else of the power of prayer; it is a conviction every person must come to for himself.

John Wisdom makes a similar point about religious belief in his famous parable of the gardener. (The parable is an analogy of the debate between theist and atheist as to whether God exists.) "Two people," Wisdom writes, "return to their long-neglected garden and find among the weeds a few old plants surprisingly vigorous. One says to the other, 'It must be that a gardener has been coming and doing something about these plants.' Upon inquiry they find that no neighbour has ever seen anyone at work in their garden. The first man says, 'He must have worked while people slept.' The other replies, 'No, someone would have heard him and besides, anyone who cares about the plants would have kept down the weeds.' The debate between these two men continues as they study the garden more carefully. Eventually however, as Wisdom explains, "the gardener hypothesis has ceased to be experimental, the difference between one who accepts and one who rejects it is not now a matter of the one expecting something the other does not expect."[25] In other words, these men are not disagreeing about the observable facts; they are disagreeing over the interpretation they give to them. So it is in the debate between the believer and non-believer concerning the efficacy of prayer. They are not discussing the observed facts - they agree about them. Their disagreement lies in whether a fulfilled or unfulfilled petitionary prayer is the cause behind the observed facts. And in this moral life there is no means of verifying or falsifying this.

---

[25] J. Wisdom: <u>Philosophy and Psychoanalysis</u>, Beverley, University of California Press, pp. 154-155.

CHAPTER 7

DIVINE WILL AND PETITIONARY PRAYERS

In Chapter 2 we examined various petitionary prayers in which God was asked to communicate in some way with the person who makes a prayer. For example in the Psalms the psalmist asked God for guidance and teaching.[1] Presumably when he asked for help not to perform an evil action,[2] the psalmist was asking for some kind of divine guidance. In Rabbinic literature this same desire is expressed. Rabbi for example wrote, "May it be Thy will, O Lord our God, and God of our fathers, to deliver us from the evil impulse." In the Prayer Book Jews pray for God's counsel. We read for example in the fourth benediction of the Amidah: "Be pleased to grant us from Thee knowledge, understanding and discernment." Again in the morning service for the Sabbath and Festivals, Jews pray: "Lord of the Universe, fulfil the prayers of my heart for good.... May it be Thy will, Lord our God, and God of our fathers, that we be privileged to do deeds that are good in Thy sight and to walk before Thee in the ways of the upright."

Since according to the Jewish tradition God communicated his guidance and knowledge through the commandments which he gave to Moses on Mt. Sinai, these prayers could be interpreted as requests for God to direct the hearts of the petitioners to divine commands. These prayers would thus contain this sentiment: "Please, God, make me aware of the commandments which you have already given to our people." They would resemble other liturgical prayers such as that found in the Amidah of the Afternoon Sabbath service: "Open my heart to

---

[1]   Psalm 25:5.

[2]   Psalm 141:4.

Thy Torah, that my soul may follow Thy commands."[3]   Though these petitions could be understood in this way, it is more likely that they were intended as requests for a communication from God.   In the case of the Psalms there is no reason to think that the psalmist was asking God to make him more aware of God's commandments which were recorded elsewhere; his prayers appear to be petitions for God's direct guidance.   Similarly when the rabbis prayed to God, they seem to be asking for some type of guidance.   And there is no doubt that frequently when Jews recite prayers in the Prayer Book, they are consciously asking for God's help in solving their personal problems; if this were not their intent, it would be difficult to understand why they formulate prayers in the way they do.   Why for example would they ask God for guidance, knowledge and wisdom, if they only want God to direct their hearts to God's commandments?   Surely they would pray (as they do elsewhere in the Jewish liturgy): "Make me cleave to Thy commandments."

When Jews pray in this manner, what exactly are they asking for?   In our daily lives we often face perplexing circumstances where it is difficult to know what to do.   A wife for instance might pray: "Please God, help me to find a way to communicate with my husband."   Or when a child finds himself isolated from his friends, he might say: "Please God, make them like me."   Or a bereaved husband might offer this prayer after his wife's death: "God, I need your help.   Help me to find new meaning in my life; guide me so that I will know how to face my life alone."   When such divine guidance is requested, Jewish sources sometimes portray God communicating His response.   We read for example that after Abraham petitioned God to spare the city of Sodom, He responded, "If I find in the city of Sodom

---

3   Daily Prayer Book, New York, Hebrew Publishing Co., 1949, p. 460.

fifty good men, I will pardon the whole place for their sake."[4]
Regardless whether such a passage is to be understood
anthropomorphically, the author clearly believed that God
communicated His willingness to comply with Abraham's request.
Here and elsewhere in the Jewish tradition there is the implicit
assumption that God can and does communicate His guidance in
response to prayer. Furthermore, there is the belief that such
counsel should be accepted. Asking God for guidance is not like
asking human beings. We might ask a friend for advice, but we
are under no obligation to accept it. This however is not the
case when we petition God.

But why should we do what God says? In Applications of
Moral Philosophy: R.M. Hare explains: "I can only conclude," he
writes, "that I ought to do it (what God wills me to do) if I am
given the additional premise that God wills that and that only
to be done, which ought to be done.... Only if we are given the
moral premise, 'X [God] wills that and that only to be done,
which ought to be done' can we, from this, in conjunction with
the premise 'X's [God's] will is, that I do A,' conclude that I
ought to do A."[5] In other words, Hare maintains that it is only
when we add to the minor premise "God commanded that I do
such and such" the major premise "God commands that and that
only to be done which ought to be done" that we are entitled to
draw the conclusion: "I ought to do such and such." Since the
validity of this deduction depends on the truth of the major
premise, what is the basis for making the assertion, "God
commands that and that only to be done, which ought to be
done"? According to Hare, this additional premise is one which
believers "all accept because they believe that God is good; and
part of what we mean by saying that God is good is that He

---

4   Genesis 18:26.

5   R.M. Hare: Applications of Moral Philosophy, London,
Macmillan, 1972, p. 4.

wills that and that only to be done which ought to be done."[6]
Throughout Jewish sources God's goodness is continually
affirmed. For example, in Exodus 34:6, God is described as "a
God compassionate and gracious, long-suffering, ever constant
and true, maintaining constancy to thousands, forgiving iniquity,
rebellion, and sin." In Rabbinic literature we read that "just as
God's love extends to humans, so His mercy is upon the cattle
and birds."[7] In the same vein R. Jannai quoted the words of R.
Gamaliel who asserted, "A man buys a pound of meat. How
much trouble and pain does it cause him till he sees it cooked.
I, God, cause wind to blow, clouds to lift, rain and dew to
descend, plants to grow and ripen, a table is ready before
everyone, all the creatures get all they need, each person
according to his requirements."[8] Similarly, R. Akiba wrote,
"There is no arbitrariness in God's deeds. The words of Him
'who spake, and the world was created,' cannot be refuted. He
judges everything in truth and justice."[9] Coupled with the
attributes of goodness and justice is the belief that God is the
source of truth. In Psalm 15:2 God is called the "God of
Truth," and this attribute is further elaborated in the Rabbinic
sources. We read in the Talmud that the "seal of the Holy One
Blessed by He is Truth."[10]

According to the Bible and the rabbis, God is all-good and
thus wills only that which ought to be done. But if God
commands what ought to be done, does He do so because what
He commands is intrinsically right? Or is what He commands

---

6   Ibid. p. 3.

7   Deut. R. 6:1.

8   Marmorstein: The Old Rabbinic Doctrine of God, p.
198.

9   Makh. 33a.

10   Sanh. 64a.

right because it has been commanded by God? In other words, is the fact that God has commanded that a particular action be performed sufficient to make that action right? This issue raises a difficult problem concerning divine communication. Jews believe God can and does communicate His guidance in response to prayer. They also think that because of their belief about God's nature, any guidance which God gives must necessarily be followed. But what is the believer to do if he believes that in response to prayer God has given morally repugnant guidance? For example he might pray: "God, please guide me. I want to serve you. But I don't know what to do. Please tell me how I can serve you best." Such a heartfelt prayer would be the expression of deep religious feeling and commitment. But what would be the response of the person who made such a prayer if he believed that God replied: "There is only one thing I ask of you, I want you to kill your son. Take him and sacrifice him. That will be a sufficient sign of your dedication and faith." Of course the believer might argue that God would never make such a demand, but did He not do just that to Abraham? He said, "Take your son Isaac, your only son, whom you love and go to the land of Moriah. There you shall offer him as a sacrifice on one of the hills which I will show you."[11]

How is one to decide whether to do this? If God did command someone to sacrifice his son, presumably such an action would be morally right - after all the presupposition behind prayers for guidance is that God only commands what ought to be done. It seems therefore that God's guidance is right because it is offered by Him. Yet it could be argued that the fact that it is God who has offered guidance does not make what He says morally acceptable. Rather God only commands those actions which are moral in and of themselves. Since this

---

[11]   Genesis 22:2.

is so, it makes no sense to think that God would tell someone to engage in human sacrifice. If we accept that God would never act in this way we are confronted with two dilemmas. First, how do we know what God has commanded? In the Bible we read of men being guided by God to do some appalling things; how do we judge whether the guidance is really good enough to have come from God? Of course we might rely on what our consciences tell us. This is H.D. Lewis' point when he writes, "We read of God in parts of the Bible... as instigating men to actions which are most repugnant to our own consciences, actions which it seems thus impossible to ascribe to the initiative of a supreme and perfect Being. When we say this we are in some fashion judging the Bible; and however presumptuous that may appear, it is very hard to avoid it in the present form."[12] Our consciences however are part of us; they are human and fallible and may make mistakes in judging the validity of divine guidance. So we are left with uncertainty about the standards by which we can judge whether an alleged divine communication is in fact from God. In other words, if God offers only guidance which conforms to intrinsically moral standards, then it is unclear precisely what such standards are and how we can be sure that we know them.[13]

The second difficulty concerns the process of divine revelation. It has been assumed that divine communication is a process by which God discloses either Himself or a body of truths and commandments. In the words of H.D. Lewis, "the idea of revelation is the idea of something which is being shown more strictly, unveiled or unfolded. This is usually thought to happen in religion by the initiative of some agent who makes himself known in this way. In revelation then God shows us

---

[12]   H.D. Lewis: Philosophy of Religion, London, University Press Ltd., 1965, p. 233.

[13]   P. Geach: God and the Soul, London, Routledge & Kegan Paul, 1969, p. 120.

what He is like and what He requires of us."[14]   If through revelation God discloses what He requires of us, it is possible that God may desire to disclose new information.   It may be that God wants to teach human beings a moral code different from the one they possess.   How could God do this if His divine communication is to be evaluated on the basis of the moral code which God seeks to replace.   (There would be no way for God to convince those to whom He revealed such a moral system that they were in fact receiving an authentic revelation - they would refuse to believe that they were experiencing a real revelation if it conflicted with the moral standards they accepted on other grounds.)   Given such a situation, how could God communicate new moral insights conflicting with the standards human beings have come to accept?   We know that the adoption of a moral system by an individual or by a group is a matter of historical circumstances and ·cannot lay claim to perfection.   Yet on this view alleged divine communications would be accepted only as long as they conformed to the moral standards of those who received them.

In the book of Deuteronomy, the author asks how we could recognize an authentic divine disclosure: "How shall we recognise a word that the Lord has not uttered?"   In response, the text states: "This is the answer: When the word spoken by the prophet in the name of the Lord is not fulfilled and does not come true, it is not a word spoken by the Lord."[15] Further, "when a prophet or dreamer appears among you and offers a sign or a portent and calls on you to follow other gods whom you have not known and worship them, even if the sign or portent should come true, do not listen to the words of that prophet or that dreamer... that prophet or that dreamer... has preached rebellion against the Lord your God... he has tried to

---

[14]   Lewis: Philosophy of Religion, p. 227.

[15]   Deut. 13:1-5.

lead you astray from the path which the Lord your God commanded you to take."[16]   So, a prophet who advocates worshipping other gods or a prophet who predicts an event which does not subsequently occur, is discredited. In terms of Rabbinical jurisprudence, this view was elaborated to include in the class of false prophets those who proclaim that Jewish law does not have to be observed, or who proclaim that they have received revelations which change the law.[17]   This view stipulates that God only communicates with men in conformity with these principles. But we are driven back to ask how we can be certain that God has in fact revealed Jewish law. The view that any alleged revelation which contradicts the Jewish legal code is by definition not an authentic revelation is derived from the belief that what is contained in Jewish law has been revealed by God. What is the basis of this belief? If one replies: "This assertion is based on God's statement in Scripture that He revealed the Jewish legal code," one merely pushes the discussion back one stage. Our initial question remains unanswered. As Lewis writes, "An authority must produce its credentials. We do not accept it at random."[18]

At the heart of this discussion is the question how can we ever be sure that we have received a divine disclosure. We have seen that perplexing problems arise form the belief that God reveals in answer to prayer only those commandments which are intrinsically moral, and from the belief that God only reveals those commandments which conform to Jewish law. Yet equally bewildering problems arise in connection with the very concept of divine revelation. Let us begin with an examination of the process and nature of God's communication. According to some theologians, God's revelation is understood as a process

---

16   Deut. 13:1-5.

17   Jewish Encyclopaedia, Vol. 10, p. 212.

18   Lewis: Philosophy of Religion, p. 234.

by which divinely authenticated propositions are disclosed. This seems to be the view of the Biblical authors. Other writers interpret revelation as a process of Divine disclosure in which God Himself is encountered. From this standpoint propositions are not revealed, but are the fruit of human attempts to formulate the significance of revelatory events. According to John Hick, "this non-propositional conception of revelation is connected with the recent renewed emphasis upon the personal character of God, and the thought that the divine-human personal relationship consists in something more than the promulgation and reception of theological truths."[19] If revelation is not a disclosure of true propositions, what is it? According to H.H. Farmer, "wheresoever and whensoever God declares Himself to the individual soul in such wise that He is apprehended as holy will actively present within the immediate situation, asking obedience at all costs and guaranteeing in and through asking the soul's ultimate succour, there is revelation. The essential content of revelation is, therefore, rightly said to be God Himself, and not general truths about God or the universe, or immortality or the way of duty..."[20] Only through such a divine disclosure is it possible to formulate propositional statements about God, the world, moral actions, and so on. "Such truths," Farmer writes, "are implicit in the divine self-giving."[21]

These two basic conceptions of revelation as they relate to prayer are beset with difficulties. If we accept the first theory (that God reveals propositions to mankind in response to petitionary prayers), how can we be certain that God does in fact act in this way? In the Bible, Rabbinic literature, and in

---

[19] Ibid. p. 70.

[20] H.H. Farmer: The World and God, London, Nisbet & Co. Ltd., 1935, p. 88.

[21] Ibid.

the daily lives of many Jews, God is described as communicating His will.   But how can we ascertain whether these accounts are true?   This question is similar to the question posed in the last chapter: "How can we be sure that God answers all petitionary prayers?"   Both questions are appeals for evidence.   But if it is true here (as it was in the case of the assertion that "God answers all petitionary prayers") that there is no clear evidence to support this claim, should we abandon the belief that God acts in this fashion?   For believers, this is not an insurmountable obstacle.   The devout believe that the lack of evidence available to support their religious convictions is not a problem.   In this regard Dorothy Emmet writes that "faith is distinguished from the entertainment of a probable proposition by the fact that the latter can be a completely theoretic affair. Faith is a 'yes' of self-commitment, it does not turn probabilities into certainties; only a sufficient increase in the weight of evidence could do that.   But it is a volitional response which takes us out of the theoretic attitude."[22]   Faith is not a matter of theoretical testing; it is instead based on a commitment determined by a deliberate act of the will.   In other words, religious belief (unlike other beliefs we have about the world) is not made on the basis of observation and testing.

It should be noted however that the claim "God communicates with men in response to prayer" is different from the statement "God answers all petitionary prayers," which is untestable in principle.   The proposition "God communicates with men in response to petitionary prayer" is based on a very special sort of evidence.   A divine disclosure of true propositions is empirical in the sense that any verbal communication is.   If I state that my wife just spoke to me, I would make such a claim because I actually heard her voice- such experience is the empirical basis of my statement.

---

[22] D. Emmet: The Nature of Metaphysical Thinking, London, Macmillan, 1945, p. 140.

Similarly if I assert that God communicated with me in the sense of revealing propositions, my claim would be supported by my experience of such a revelation. If God's communication is understood as propositional in character, a believer might assert that God spoke to him. For example in the Bible when God spoke to Abraham concerning the fate of Sodom, this disclosure could be viewed as a verbal transmission. Some believers might stress that such Divine communication is private; it was only revealed to Abraham. But if the experience of divine revelation is subjective, how can one check up on it? As Thomas Hobbes explained, "if any man pretend to me that God hath spoken to him... I make doubt of it, I cannot easily perceive what argument he can produce to oblige me to believe it. To say He hath spoken to him in a dream, is no more than to say that he dreamed that God spoke to him.... So that though God almighty can speak to a man by dreams, visions, voice, and inspiration; yet he obliges no man to believe he hath done so to him that pretends it; who (being a man) may err, and (which is more) may lie."[23] Because a man had certain subjective experiences, we cannot conclude that these experiences are of what is really the case. For example, the fact that Amos thought that God spoke to him after he prayed for God to forgive Israel does not guarantee the validity of his belief. And even if Amos had undergone a dramatic transformation as a result of this experience, we would not be entitled to conclude that God had actually spoken to him -he might just as well have been changed for other reasons.

Quite apart from this, there is the issue of religious pluralism. In the religious traditions of the world, numerous individuals have claimed that they heard gods communicate with them in response to prayer. How could such revelations have taken place if they frequently contradict one another? The

---

23   Thomas Hobbes: Leviathan, Chapter 32.

difficulty is not made any easier by the fact that individuals claim they have received revelations only from gods within their own traditions. As Flew points out, one would be astounded "to hear of the vision of Bernadette Souburois occurring not to a Roman Catholic at Lourdes but to a Hindu in Benares, or of Apollo manifest not in classical Delphi but in Kyoto under the Shoguns."[24]   The fact that adherents of a particular religious faith always believe that divine communications come from the god or gods of their particular tradition raises the question whether such communications are simply figments of their imagination.

It might be objected that divine communications do not need any external criteria to validate them.   They are self-authenticating.   In other words, the subjective experiences of those who believe they have received divine communications contain some type of marks or guarantee that they are actually communications from God.   In World and God, H.H. Farmer expressed this idea as follows: "the... experience of God as personal, which in the nature of the case must be self-authenticating and able to shine in its own light independently of the abstract reflections of philosophy, for if it were not, it could hardly be a living experience of God as personal."   This claim puts any alleged divine communication beyond the range of analysis and criticism.   But such an explanation leaves open the question how we are able to determine which communications are from God.   If one individual claims that God communicated one thing in response to prayer, and another person believes that God communicated the opposite, how are we to determine which (if either) was from God?   If a believer contends that he received a communication from the god of his religious tradition, but an individual from a different religion claims that he received the opposite information from a different god, how can

_____

24   A. Flew: God and Philosophy, London, Hutchinson and Co., 1966, p. 127.

we determine who is right? The criterion of self-authentication does not help us. The major problem with the idea of self-authentication is that those who have defended the validity of divine communications on this basis have not specified those marks which authenticate them. Those who hold the view that divine revelation is self-authenticating, do so because they believe that their subjective religious experiences refer to objective reality. Yet they render their assertions immune to observation and testing. Again we are faced with the same problem we discussed with regard to the verification and falsification of religious beliefs. We must accept that we can never know for certain whether an individual's claim to have received a divine communication in response to prayer is valid. Since it is not based on clear evidence, it cannot be firmly established.

What are we to say about the second conception of revelation where God is thought of as revealing Himself? This notion of revelation is based on the analogy of a close human relationship. We do not make judgements about individuals wholly or even partly on the basis of what they tell us about themselves. We have personal experiences of them and form our judgements on this basis. Similarly those who subscribe to the second conception of divine revelation conceive of God revealing Himself - propositions about Him are merely deductions made by the individual as a result of an encounter. This notion of revelation has the same difficulty as the idea of propositional revelation - if I say that in response to my prayer, God directly revealed Himself to me, how can I be sure that I really did have such an experience? There is another difficulty with this notion. Suppose an individual were having difficulty in his marriage and went to see his local marriage counsellor. If the counsellor were of the old school, he would probably give the man some direct advice about his marriage; he would try to give some ideas on how to remedy the situation, keep his wife happy, and so on. If the counsellor were somewhat younger and more progressive, he would probably go in for "non-directive" counselling. He would listen sympathetically, nod his head, say, "um... yes I see...," and try to help the man by giving him the opportunity to sort out his own thoughts. However, if in desperation the husband turned to him and said, "But what would you do if you were in my position?" the counsellor would probably give a truthful answer. Even if he refused to do so, the husband would get quite a good idea from his body movements, his facial expression, and his general attitude. Suppose however instead of going to a marriage guidance counsellor, the husband prayed to God to help him in his difficulties. If the non-propositional view of revelation is correct, then although God can reveal Himself He would not express in separate propositions what the poor man should do. It would be like going to the non-directive marriage counsellor; the only difference is that since the husband would believe that God is incorporeal, he could not make deductions from any facial expressions or body movements. Thus it seems that if the non-propositional notion of revelation is true, it is difficult to understand how God answers such a prayer as this husband's.

Suppose however the next day the husband tripped, fell down the stairs and broke his leg. A believer in revelation might argue that as God supposedly revealed Himself non-propositionally in events in the Bible, so the husband's accident was God's answer to his prayer. But how exactly is the accident to be interpreted? Perhaps the husband should stay at home and be nursed by his wife so that they get to know one another better. But how is he to know that this is what God wants? Perhaps what God is really telling him is that he should go and stay in the hospital to get out of his wife's hair. And, to add perplexity to perplexity, how does the husband know whether the accident was the answer to prayer anyway? There is a further difficulty above and beyond this. Jews believe that

God is omnipotent; then clearly, He is able to reveal His will to men. But if He is able to reveal His will, why has He allowed so much confusion about the contents of His communication. Why does He not make Himself clear? Such confusion could be due to the fact that God reveals Himself according to the theory of non-propositional revelation in ways that could easily be misinterpreted. However even on the view that God communicates His guidance in terms of propositions, there is a wide divergence of opinion concerning exactly what God has communicated. If God wants people to follow His guidance, why does He allow such confusion to exist? It may be the case that God does not want to force human beings to observe His commandments in order that they might have free will, but this does not explain why God would not clearly indicate what His wishes are.

To sum up, we can see that if we ask God for guidance in our daily lives, we come up against some fearful problems. Suppose we believe God tells us what to do and we feel that His advice is morally wrong, how can we know whether we should follow that advice or conclude that it was really not from God? Even if we believe that God has given us advice of which we approve, our problems are not over; how can we be sure it is in fact of divine origin? Suppose He is not a God who gives advice; suppose revelation is a non-propositional encounter with the Divine, does it make sense then to ask Him for help in the first place if there is such uncertainty about what He would want us to do? Finally, if he is a loving and all-powerful God, surely He would want to help us. Why then does He leave us so confused?

CHAPTER 8

THE ACCEPTABILITY OF PETITIONARY PRAYERS

There are many prayers in the Jewish liturgy which seem acceptable at face value such as the fourth benediction of the Amidah ("Be pleased to grant us from Thee knowledge, understanding, and discernment"), and the eighth benediction of the Amidah ("Heal us, O Lord, and we shall be healed"). These prayers are requests for human welfare and therefore consonant with God's benevolence. Conversely there are some prayers in the Bible which appear unacceptable such as the psalmist prayer for God to punish his enemies.[1] According to Lewis, such a prayer is unworthy and ought to be rejected: "Not every prayer," he writes, "is for a sufficiently worthy end. Men do sometimes pray for ends which it is preposterous to expect God to bless in any way. If I pray for terrible destruction to fall on my enemy or request that fire from heaven should consume those who oppose me, then I am seeking God's co-operation in matters not consistent with His character and declared purpose.... One certainly ought not to pray for preferential treatment which would place others at an unjust disadvantage."[2] Thus, he concludes, "a vast number of unanswered prayers will fall into the class of prayers for radically unworthy ends which it is wrong, indeed blasphemous and not merely ill-judged, to make the subject of prayer."[3]

How does Lewis know that such prayers are never granted? If I pray that God unwarrantedly punish someone and no punishment is forthcoming, it may be that my prayer was not efficacious because I prayed for God to act contrary to His nature. But what evidence is there to support this claim? Of course, there is the evidence that what I prayed for did not

---

[1]   Psalm 70:2-3.

[2]   Lewis: Our Experience of God, p. 259.

[3]   Ibid. pp. 258-259.

occur. But this could have just as easily been a coincidence. The fact that what I prayed for did not occur is a necessary, but not a sufficient condition for its efficacy. Again, suppose I prayed for God to harm an individual and he subsequently contracted an incurable illness. In such a case, Lewis would want to say that this was a coincidence which had nothing to do with my prayer. What evidence could he have in support of this view?

In addition to prayers for unworthy ends, Lewis maintains that "prayers for trivial ends or things we can quite properly provide for ourselves" also fall into the class of "unanswered prayers." He writes: "We have been set to live in a certain kind of world, and to ask at every point that the normal conditions of existence be altered to suit our immediate convenience is to rebel against the wisdom of God in creating just this sort of world and to repudiate our own responsibilities."[4] No doubt Lewis is right in thinking that we should not continually ask God for what we are too lazy to provide for ourselves. To conceive a God as the genie in Aladdin's lamp would be grossly to misrepresent His nature. Yet it is questionable whether Lewis is correct in insisting that prayers for simple and ordinary concerns are in principle unacceptable. Who is to determine what is a trivial end? Certainly, many of the prayers we considered in Chapter 2 might appear to be of minimal significance (such as Jacob's prayer for good and clothing, Samson's prayer for something to drink, and Rabbi's prayer to be delivered from a hard lawsuit). Throughout the Jewish liturgy there is no discrimination made between what might seem to be trivial and weighty matters. Further just in the case of prayers for unworthy ends, we have no basis for determining whether prayers for seemingly trivial ends are unanswered and thereby unacceptable.

---

4   Ibid. p. 259.

Another form of petitionary prayer which falls into the category of "unanswered prayers," according to Lewis, are prayers which are "made in a casual and light-hearted or thoughtless manner."[5]   Again, there would be no way to demonstrate that such prayers go unanswered.   But there is a further problem.   Lewis argues that a prayer is unacceptable if it is offered without proper solemnity and sincerity.   In other words Lewis believes that for a prayer to be granted it must be offered sincerely.   For example if I recite prayers contained in the Jewish Prayer Book without thinking about their meaning or without really caring if they are granted, then for Lewis such prayers could be of no avail.   Yet if Lewis is right, then it appears that the frame of mind of the person who offers a prayer is more important than the prayer itself - on this account God would seem to be more interested in the attitude of the person praying than in what is being prayed for.   Assume there is someone in the hospital whom I dislike.   A relative might ask me to pray for him, or I might be asked at a religious service to join in the congregational prayer for this person's recovery.   If I did pray for this person, my prayer might well be said in a thoughtless or insincere way.   For Lewis, a prayer said in this manner could not be efficacious. Does it make sense to think that God would be more concerned with my attitude than in the recovery of the person for whom I am praying?   Lewis also writes that "if we look to reputed cases of answers to prayer... and especially to notable ones such as those which have prominence in sacred scriptures and the lives of conspicuously holy men, we may indeed find that there is much which may be treated as coincidence or superstitious legend; but we may nonetheless also find an impressive correlation of such occurrences and the peculiar enlivening of

---

5   Ibid. p. 260.

the sense of God."[6]   Here Lewis is arguing that in some cases where there has been such an experience, prayers have been answered.   What does this enlivening event consist of? Unfortunately Lewis does not explain.

Like Lewis various rabbis distinguished between acceptable and unacceptable prayers.   R. Eliezer for example argued that if a person prays without paying attention to what he is saying, thereby making his prayer a fixed taste, his prayer is not supplication, and thereby unacceptable.[7]   Conversely, other types of prayers were believed to be acceptable, some more so than others.   We read for example that a man should not only pray for himself but should also think of others using the plural form "grant us" rather than the singular form "grant me."[8]   The rabbis also asserted that "if a man needs something for himself but prays to God to grant that very thing to his neighbour who needs it, such an unselfish prayer causes God to grant him his wish first."[9]

If some petitionary prayers are acceptable and others unacceptable, how are the two to be distinguished?   It seems reasonable to think that petitionary prayers for God to perform actions which are consonant with His moral nature are in principle acceptable.   Since God is described as just, truthful, and benevolent, it would be consistent to ask Him to perform actions which are good.   For example, if I pray in the Sabbath Amidah "O grant peace, happiness, blessing, grace, kindness and mercy to us," such a prayer should be acceptable.   The fact that God is understood as having commanded that this prayer be recited during the worship service is another reason why it would be suitable.   Nevertheless there are some situations where

---

6   Ibid. p. 262.

7   Ber. 4:4.

8   Ber. 29b-30a.

9   B.K. 92a.

such prayers might not be granted. In those cases where two conflicting requests are made to God, He would in all likelihood choose to grant the most altruistic prayer. This does not mean that the other prayer is unacceptable in principle; it would simply be the less preferable. Suppose for example, a farmer with a large family had two very bad harvests. He might pray "Let the rain fall tomorrow"; in making this prayer, he would not be asking God to do anything contrary to His nature. Suppose his neighbour simultaneously prayed for good weather so that his family could get together for a picnic. The requests made in these two cases are obviously not of equal importance and urgency; the prayer for rain to water crops so that the farmer's children will have enough food to eat is more important than his neighbour's prayer for sunshine. But since it is impossible for God simultaneously to grant both requests, a choice must be made.

What can we say about prayers for seemingly trivial ends? Should we assume, as Lewis does, that they are always unacceptable? Although it might seem to an outside observer that a particular request is for something of little importance, there is no reason to assume it could not be granted if God is not asked to act against His nature. But this does not give us licence to ask God for everything; it would be wrong to conceive of God as a servant who can fulfill every human desire. Farmer is no doubt right when he writes that "making God the servant of our ends undoubtedly points to a real and insidious danger."[10] Such a danger would be, in the words of Lewis, "to ask at every point that the normal conditions of existence be altered to suit our immediate convenience," and this would no doubt be a repudiation of our responsibilities.[11] Nevertheless if it is wrong to ask God to provide for all our needs, where is one to draw the line between an excess as

---

[10] Farmer: The World and God, p. 139.

[11] Lewis: Our Experience of God, p. 259.

against a legitimate number of demands? There seems no clear answer. When believers ask God to provide for their needs, they thereby relinquish their own responsibility to provide for themselves; they become dependent on God's will. At what point must such dependence cease? Despite this perplexity there are prayers which, though acceptable in principle, do seem unreasonable. If I am cold, I could ask God to provide me with an expensive new coat. There is nothing wrong in principle with asking God to provide me with some sort of clothing- such a request would be consonant with His beneficence. But what about a luxurious garment? Certainly any sort of clothing would be sufficient as long as it kept me warm. Thus some qualification of the claim that "all requests for God to act in accordance with His moral nature are acceptable" seems necessary. But what constitutes a reasonable demand? Intuitively some requests seem unreasonable: to ask God for a beautiful car, or a magnificent house. Yet the fact that these prayers are motivated by personal concerns does not rule them out. All petitionary prayers do this; we must find a way to differentiate between interests which are legitimate and those which are not.

Such considerations apply equally to prayers we make on behalf of others. We have seen that the rabbis believed prayers made for the welfare of others are more acceptable than prayers made for one's own benefit. It could be argued that such intercessionary prayer is acceptable since the petitioner is acting altruistically. Yet are all intercessory prayers motivated by altruism? It is not at all clear that they are. Consider the case of a son who prays for his aunt to recover from a sickness because he does not want the responsibility of caring for her. Furthermore intercessory prayers can be just as unreasonable as other prayers we have considered. For example a person might pray that his homeless parents receive a beautiful mansion staffed by servants. Although he would be asking God to perform an action consonant with His benevolence, such a request seems unreasonable because of its extravagance. Yet here as before we lack a precise criterion for determining the exact point at which a request to God is unwarranted by the circumstances.

What are we to say about those prayers which are said in a thoughtless manner? For example, I could offer intercessory prayers to God during a worship service without paying any attention to the words I was saying, or without even caring whether my requests are granted. In such a case are we to conclude that these prayers are unacceptable? Theoretically such prayers are consonant with God's nature. But if they are said in a thoughtless manner, does it follow that they are of no avail? If so, it would appear that God is more interested in the frame of mind of the petitioner rather than in the welfare of the persons who are being prayed for. This paradoxical situation raises a further question concerning the necessity of prayer. Since God commanded Jews to recite prayers for the eradication of suffering, unhappiness and so forth, such events seem to be dependent in part on the act of praying. But surely it would have been simpler for God to have eliminated such evils in the first place? Perhaps God is willing to accept any petitionary prayer which is consonant with His nature even if it is made in a thoughtless way. Such a view would overcome the dilemma how God could be more interested in the frame of mind of the person who is praying than in the welfare of the persons being prayed for. But it does raise the question how prayers which are said in a thoughtless manner, or without any concern that they be granted, could be acceptable. Surely if the recitation of petitionary prayers is no more than a mechanical process done without thought and at times without even the belief that there is a God who hears prayer, it seems implausible that they could be efficacious. If prayers are to be of avail, must they not be prayed seriously with concern that they be granted, and with the belief that they can bring results? Here we are confronted with a serious problem: on the one hand, if we believe that God would not grant those prayers which are said in a thoughtless manner, then He must be more interested in the intention of the person who is praying than in those who are being prayed for. On the other hand, if we believe that God would grant a prayer even if it were said in an insincere way, then (implausible as it may seem) petitions which are made insincerely or without any concern that they be granted are legitimate.

This dilemma also applies to those cases in which prayers are made out of selfish or malicious motives for the welfare of others. I mentioned that a nephew might pray that his aunt recover solely so that he would not have to bear the burden of financial responsibility. Could such a prayer be granted? If it is acceptable, then the motive of the person praying has nothing to do with the acceptability of the prayer. This seems odd since motives play a major role in determining whether actions are moral; should they not be of some significance in determining whether prayers are acceptable? Yet if we argue that a prayer is unacceptable because of the motive of the person praying, then the intention of the person who is praying seems more important than the welfare of the persons who are being prayed for. Can this truly be? What are we to say about those prayers which are made for the welfare of others which are made on the basis of subconsciously selfish or malicious intentions? Suppose someone prayed for his relative's recovery though in fact his action was motivated by the wish (which he repressed from himself) not to accept the financial burden of his relative's illness and incapacity. What are we to say about such a petition? (Of course in the mind of the person who made the prayer there would be no obstacle in thinking it is acceptable since it would appear to him to be made for the right reasons.) Are we to say that such a prayer is unacceptable? If so, God would appear to be more interested in the person praying (and in this case in his subconscious motives) than in the welfare of the person prayed for. Can this be?

And what are we to say about those seemingly acceptable prayers - motivated by altruism - which are requests for God to perform actions of crucial significance? For example Abraham prayed that Sodom not be destroyed; Amos prayed that Israel not be overcome, and Moses prayed for Israel to be forgiven for her sin. In all of these cases prayers were made for God to perform events of great magnitude. Are they acceptable? Arguably such prayers are not objectionable, yet they are peculiar in the sense that they presuppose that events of major significance (determining whether thousands of people will live or die) could be affected by a single person's prayer to God. How could the fate of vast numbers of people be determined in such an arbitrary way? Would it not be better if the fate of a city or a people were to be determined on the basis of the actions of those involved, rather than through prayer of supplication? As Lewis writes, "Ought not God to benefit men according to their needs or merits and not in terms of the rather haphazard and arbitrary condition of being the subject of prayer? Should momentous things, like recovery from sickness, depend on someone's asking God?"[12]

What sense can we make of the assertion that prayers offered by the righteous are more acceptable than the prayers made by wicked individuals? It might be thought that Amos' prayer for God not to destroy Israel was granted because of his virtues. Such a view is problematic. If prayers offered by the righteous are more acceptable than prayers made by those who are not, then it appears that God is more preoccupied with the moral character of those who offer prayers than in the interests of those for whom the prayers are made. For example if a malicious person involved in numerous crimes prayed for God to save his dying mother, possibly his prayer would be more acceptable if he had a moral character. But is such a situation consonant with God's benevolence?

---

12   Ibid. p. 255.

Again, if God has the moral nature ascribed to Him in the Bible, Rabbinic literature, and the Jewish Prayer Book, it is reasonable to suppose that He would not grant petitions which ask Him to act contrary to His nature. But how can we know whether the requests we make to God are, in Lewis' words, for "sufficiently worthy ends"? There are innumerable cases where it is difficult to determine whether this criterion is met. For example, what are we to say of the psalmist's prayer: "Let all who seek my life be brought to shame and dismay, let all who love to hurt me shrink back disgraced."[13] "Wilt thou not kill them (my foes)... Scatter them by thy might and bring them to ruin. Deliver them, O Lord, to be destroyed... Let them be cut off for their cursing and falsehood; bring them to an end in thy wrath, and they will be no more."[14] It does seem that God would not comply with these requests since they would require Him to act in a vindictive and merciless way. This might be the view of those who did not believe in capital punishment or who think that criminals can be re-educated through corrective punishment. Or if one believes that immoral behaviour is the product of unconscious motivations, there would be no justice in punishing those who acted immorally without a conscious awareness of what they were doing. To ask the Deity to destroy such individuals (as the psalmist desires) would run counter to God's mercy and justice.

There are other difficulties determining which prayers are legitimate. In trying to determine the rights and wrongs of a proposed course of action, it is often necessary to weigh short-term good or harm against long-term consequences, and such an evaluation cannot be made with any exactness. Information about the future course of events (which is relevant to the resolution of a moral issue) is often not obtainable to any high degree of certainty, and in some cases not at all. These factors

---

13   Psalm 70:2.

14   Psalm 59:11-13.

make it very difficult to know which actions God would refuse to carry out. Because of this uncertainty, there seems to be no way of being sure whether the requests made to God actually seek "God's co-operation in matters not consistent with His character and declared purpose."[15]   Suppose, for example, that two countries are at war with one another, and citizens of both pray: "God, let my country be victorious."   It might be that if one country were victorious its leaders would eventually be removed by a coup and immoral men take their place. Because of such a revolution, these individuals would be in a position to commit acts of injustice and violence.   It might also happen that if the other country lost the war, the rulers of the victorious country would also commit wicked acts, but less violent.   In such a situation, God would no doubt seek to avoid the worse of the two evils.   But from our limited human perspective how can we know which prayer is to be preferred? It is not merely a lack of knowledge of future events which makes it difficult to determine whether a request to God is acceptable.   If we assume that God's will is inscrutable, there is no way of knowing whether the requests we make are in fact consonant with His providence.

To sum up, the believer cannot know whether his prayers go unanswered because they are unacceptable; he has no evidence to prove this.   Furthermore, he cannot even know whether his prayers are acceptable.   How can he determine whether they are for ends so trivial or unreasonable that they are of no avail?   Even if it could be shown that they are offered thoughtlessly or selfishly, they might still be acceptable if God is more interested in what is being prayed for than in the frame of mind of the petitioner.   Moreover even if the petitioner were an evil person, his prayers could be acceptable if the aim of the prayer overshadows the character of the petitioner.   Yet we cannot know for certain how God judges

---

[15]   Lewis: Our Experience of God, p. 258.

such cases.   Finally, the believer cannot know if what he prays for is truly for the good.   Perhaps he has the wrong conception of a moral action; perhaps he is unable to evaluate all the evidence surrounding a particular situation.   And even if he does know what would be the morally correct action to take, he cannot be sure whether it would be the right course of action for God considering its potential repercussions which only God could know and in light of God's eternal plan.

CHAPTER 9

PRAYING TO GOD TO CHANGE THE PAST

One of the features of petitionary prayers contained in Jewish sources is that they are prayers for God to do something in the future. Thus Abraham asked God to give him an heir (Genesis 15: 2-3) and pleaded with Him to forgive Israel (Exodus 32: 31-32); Joshua asked God for help against Israel's enemies (Joshua 7:7); Jonah asked God to take away his life (Jonah 4: 2-3); R. Eleazar asked God to fill Israel's borders with disciples (Berakoth 16b). None of these prayers was a request to God to change the past - we never find a request of the form: "God, may it be Your will to undo what has been done." It is not inconceivable however that Jews might make a request for God to change the past. Such a prayer would resemble prayers contained in the Jewish liturgy with the striking difference that it would be formulated with respect to the past rather than the future. Thus, the eighth benediction of the Amidah, "Heal us, O Lord, and we shall be healed" is a request to God for future healing. But one could conceive of an individual who had contracted an incurable disease making a similar prayer to God to alter the past: "Heal me, Lord. Make it be that I never contracted this disease." Or an individual who lost an arm in a motor accident might pray: "Lord, let the accident not have taken place. Let me have my arm as before."

The Jewish liturgy does not contain such prayers as these, but they are discussed in the Talmud. In Berakoth 54a two prayers are mentioned in which the petitioner asked God to change the past. In the first, the petitioner said the following prayer after his wife had become pregnant: "May God grant that my wife bear a son." Since the sex of the child had been determined at conception, such a prayer would be a request for

God to change the past if the child conceived were female.[1]   In the second case, the petitioner had just come home from a journey and hearing cries of distress prayed: "May God grant that these cries do not come from my house."   If such cries did in fact come from his house, then he would be asking God to change the past in that he would be asking God to bring it about that the cries came from elsewhere.[2]

Such prayers as these should, as Peter Geach remarks, be sharply distinguished from requests which by their grammatical form may be taken as requests for an action to take place in the past.   A teacher for example might say to his student, "Have your essay written by Tuesday morning."   "But," as Geach points out, "this does not make sense of the sort of imperative that would be used in praying about the past.   The indicative corresponding to the teacher's imperative is 'You will have written your essay by Tuesday morning'; and this is not in the past tense.   It is in the tense aptly called by old grammarians 'paulo post futurum'; it relates to a time somewhere between the time of speaking and the following Tuesday morning – and thus to a time which is future, not past, when the teacher speaks, though by the Tuesday morning it will be a past time."[3]

Could such prayers be efficacious?   According to Geach, they could not.   "A prayer certainly does not make sense," he writes, "if we try to use a past tense of the imperative mood... In using the imperative we represent the situation as still to be brought about, and in using the past tense we represent it as already a <u>fait accompli</u> one way or other.   These representations will not fit together; such a prayer makes no better sense than

---

1   Berakoth, 54a.

2   <u>Ibid</u>.

3   Geach: <u>God and the Soul</u>, p. 90.

a schoolboy's prayer for...(a number) to have the value he gave it in his maths test - 3.1416 or 3.1461, as the case may be."[4]

But if God is omnipotent, is there anything wrong in asking Him to act in this way? If for God all things are possible, presumably there would be no objection in thinking that He could change past occurrences. Omnipotence might appear to embrace all action, as Aquinas writes.

"Can God make what had been not to have been? It seems that He can, for what is impossible in itself is much more impossible than what is impossible under the circumstances. God can do what is impossible in itself, like giving sight to a blind man, or raising a corpse to life. Much more, therefore, can He do what is impossible under the circumstances. For a thing in the past not to have happened is impossible under the circumstances or incidentally; for instance, that Socrates happened not to have run from the fact that he did. So God can make what has happened not to have happened. Moreover, whatever God could have done he can do now, since his power has not diminished. But God could have seen to it that before Socrates was going to run he would not run. Therefore after he had run God could effect that he had not run."[5]

How could God do this? We constantly affect the future by our decisions, our actions, and our influence over others, but we cannot change the past. There is simply no way for us to affect events that have already taken place. But if God is able to affect past events, he must both perceive the past and act differently from human beings. One explanation of the way in which God could act in this manner is offered by C.S. Lewis in

4   Ibid.

5   Aquinas: Summa Theologica, Vol. 5, p. 167.

<u>Miracles</u>. According to Lewis, God stands outside time and sees the whole pattern of events in time which are subject to His will. Therefore God can shape an event that comes earlier to fit in with a prayer that comes later. "It is probable," Lewis writes, "that Nature is not really in Time and almost certain that God is not. Time is probably (like perspective) the mode of our perception. There is therefore in reality no question of God's at one point in time (the moment of creation) adapting the material history of the universe in advance to free acts which you or I are to perform at a later point in Time. To Him all the physical events and all the human acts are present in an eternal Now."[6]

To explain this theory, Lewis uses the analogy of a designer who draws a pattern of lines on a piece of paper. "Suppose," he writes, "I find a piece of paper on which a black line is already drawn.... Let us now suppose that the original black line is conscious.... Let us also give this black line free will.... The particular wavy shape of it is the shape it wills to have. But whereas it is aware of its own chosen shape only moment by moment.... I can see its shape as a whole and all at once.... I can now sit down and draw other lines (say in red) so shaped as to combine with the black line into a pattern."[7] Lewis continues by stating that at every moment I will find my red lines waiting for the black line and adapted to it. In composing the total red-and-black design, I have the whole course of the black line in view and take it into account. "In this model," he writes, "the black line represents a creature with free will, the red lines represent material events, and I represent God... it will be seen that if the black line addressed prayers to me I might (if I chose) grant them." Since I would

---

6   C.S. Lewis: <u>Miracles</u>, New York, Macmillan, 1971, p. 183.

7   <u>Ibid</u>.

be aware of the entire course of the black line, it is possible that if the black line prayed to me at a certain point of the line (point N, for example), I would be able to answer its prayer on the basis of a picture of the entire pattern: "For his whole course has been visible to me from the moment I looked at the paper and his requirements at point N are among the things I took into account in deciding the total pattern."[8] On the basis of this account, Lewis asserts, "... shocking as it may sound, I conclude that we can at noon become part causes of an event occurring at ten o'clock."[9] The fact that I made my prayer after the event had taken place is of no consequence since God, because He was aware that I would in the future make my prayer, took my prayer into account in determining the event.

There are serious objections to this analysis. The notion of a conscious line endowed with free will does not make sense. What does it mean to say that a line could make a petitionary prayer? How could lines represent material objects? Of course Lewis is not suggesting that geometrical lines actually possess consciousness and free will; he only wishes to draw a parallel between this particular geometrical example and God's knowledge of events. Nonetheless we know that lines simply do not operate in the way which Lewis describes, and his analogy collapses because it contains elements which are utterly fantastic. A second criticism of Lewis' view is that if time does not exist in the world from God's point of view, then either (a) God is unaware of the temporal aspects of things, which is so important to us; or (b) the temporal aspect of things is an illusion – God perceives events as simultaneous because they are in fact so. On the former view, if God is not aware of the temporal aspects of things, He is not omniscient. On the latter, since God sees events stripped of their temporal aspect, we must

---

8 Ibid. p. 184.

9 Ibid. p. 186.

see them otherwise than as they really are: our conviction that things exist temporally is a mistake. But, as Peter Strawson points out, if my impression of the temporal aspect of things is illusory, the fact that I have different and combinable illusions shows that at least illusions are successive - that they are not all present together, but now one illusion is present and now another. Whether entities A, B, and C really are events in succession or are only misperceived as such if an observer has the experience of remembering A, perceiving B to happen, and expecting C, and also has the experience of remembering that A happened before B happened and perceiving C, then these two experiences of the observer are uncombinable, and cannot occur in him simultaneously, but only successively.[10] From this discussion it is clear that these two possibilities ((a) God is unaware of the temporal aspects of things, and (b) the temporal aspects of things is an illusion) lead to serious problems. The first alternative leads to the inference that God is not omniscient; the second is beset with logical difficulties. Thus Lewis' interpretation of ex post facto petitionary prayers appears misguided.

Let us turn to the opinions of Jewish writers who believe that prayers for God to change the past are of no avail. In considering such petitionary prayers, the rabbis of the Talmud declared: "To cry over the past is to utter a vain prayer."[11] What was their reasoning? Unfortunately they gave no answer why such prayers could not be efficacious. However in Understanding Jewish Prayer G.J. Blidstein conjectures what the rabbis' argument might have been. "There is no suggestion," he writes, "that prayer possesses a potency beyond the scope of the

---

10   P. Strawson (Ed.): Studies in the Philosophy of Thought and Action, London, O.U.P., 1968, pp. 178-179.

11   Berakoth, 60a.

operative natural law."[12]   Thus, he concludes, the Talmud states that one cannot pray for a miracle.[13]   As Blidstein notes, it would be a violation of "natural law" for God to change the past.   The difficulty with this interpretation is that in this very passage the rabbis asserted: "If one sees a place where miracles have been wrought for Israel, he should say, 'Blessed be He who wrought miracles for our ancestors in this place'."[14]   By condemning prayers for God to change the past, the rabbis were not objecting to the fact that God was being asked to perform miracles; rather they were objecting to miraculous events of a special nature in which past events would have to be undone. This point is emphasized in the discussion in the Talmud concerning the prayer: "May God grant that my wife bear a son."   In this discussion, R. Joseph cited a counter example from the Bible to refute the general rule stated in the Mishnah that prayers for God to change the past are not efficacious.   In Gen. 30:21 ("And afterwards she bore a daughter, and called her name Dinah"), he noted that the expression "afterwards" indicates that although the child was conceived as a male, it was subsequently changed into a girl.   Rab made R. Joseph's objection explicit in elaborating the meaning of this term.   According to Rab, the meaning of the word "afterwards" refers to the period after Leah had passed judgement on herself, saying, "Twelve tribes are destined to issue from Jacob.   Six issued from me and four from the handmaids, making ten.   If this child will be a male, my sister Rachel will not be equal to one of the handmaids." Forthwith the child was turned into a girl.[15]   According to Rab, R. Joseph's objection is invalid because he did not understand

---

12   Petuchowski (Ed.): <u>Understanding Jewish Prayer</u>, p. 114.

13   <u>Ibid</u>.

14   Berakoth 54a.

15   Berakoth 60a.

that the sex of the child did not actually change. What occurred was that Leah made this statement about the sex of the child during the forty days of conception during which time the sex of the child was undetermined. Therefore R. Joseph was mistaken in thinking that this example refuted the general rule that petitionary prayers for God to change the past are of no avail. God did not change the sex of the child because the sex was undetermined when Leah expressed the wish that her child be a girl. Although Rab declared: "We cannot cite a miraculous event in refutation of the Mishnah," what he is saying is not that miracles never occur, but only that as a matter of principle one cannot refute the Mishnah by citing one miraculous event. Thus R. Joseph was incorrect in thinking that his example from Genesis was an instance of God's changing the past.

Why did the rabbis of the Talmud hold this view? In the Guide of the Perplexed Maimonides poses one solution. In his discussion of the nature of God's omnipotence, he asserted that although God is all-powerful, there are certain actions that He cannot perform because they are logically impossible. One of these actions, he believed, was to change the past:

"That which is impossible has a permanent and constant property, which is not the result of some agent, and cannot in any way change, and consequently we do not ascribe to God the power of doing what is impossible... all philosophers consider that it is impossible for one substratum to have at the same moment two opposite properties, or for the elementary components of a thing, substance and accident, to interchange, so that the substance becomes accident, and the accident becomes substance, or for a material substance to be without accident. Likewise it is impossible that God should produce a being like Himself, or annihilate, corporify, or change Himself. The power of God is not assumed to extend to any of these impossibilities... it is impossible to produce a square with a diagonal equal to one of its sides, or a solid angle that includes four right angles, or similar things... we have thus shown that according to each one of the different theories there are things which are impossible, whose existence cannot be admitted, and whose creation is excluded from the power of God, and the assumption that God does not change their nature does not imply weakness in God, or a limit to His power."[16]

Here Maimonides asserted that the fact that God cannot do what is logically impossible does not indicate any deficiency. Similarly Rabbi Ezra ben Solomon (a thirteenth-century Spanish kabbalist) wrote in his commentary on the Song of Songs that "the Creator, Blessed be He, similarly (to the demiurge in Plato's Timaeus) formed heaven and earth from primordial matter and sometimes something else. But it is not a deficiency on His part that the Creator, Blessed be He, is not able to create something out of nothing. Likewise, the fact that God is unable to bring about what is logically absurd, e.g. creating a square the diagonal of which is equal in length to one of its sides, or asserting and denying the same proportion, does not indicate any deficiency in God's power. Just as this does not indicate any deficiency in His power, so the fact that God cannot cause an emanation of something from nothing does not indicate that God is deficient in any way. This, also, would be logically absurd."[17]

Maimonides and Rabbi Ezra ben Solomon argued that the actions which God cannot perform are those actions which are logically inconsistent. For Maimonides such impossible actions

<hr>

16 Maimonides: The Guide of the Perplexed, New York, Hebrew Publishing Co., 1881, Part III, pp. 59-61.

17 Ezra Ben Solomon: Perush Al Shir Ha-Shirim, Altona, 1764, p. 6a.

include physical, geometrical, and mathematical impossibilities as well as theological impossibilities such as God producing a being like Himself, annihilating Himself, etc.... Ezra ben Solomon extended the concept of "impossible" actions to include creatio ex nihilo. Although these two writers did not entirely agree, they nevertheless concur that God cannot bring about a situation in which two contradictory propositions are both true. Maimonides wrote that "it is impossible for one substratum to have at the same moment two opposite properties. For example, it would be impossible for a surface to be simultaneously concave and convex." Similarly Rabbi Ezra ben Solomon asserted that it is impossible for God simultaneously to assert and deny the same proposition. Aquinas in Summa Theologica expressed the same view. In answer to the question, "Is God omnipotent?" he answered, "when you say that God has the power for everything, you are most correctly interpreted as meaning this: that since power is relative to what is possible, divine power can do everything that is possible, and on this account is called omnipotent.... Now it is incompatible with the meaning of absolutely possible that anything involving the contradiction of simultaneously being and not being should fall under divine omnipotence.... Whatever does not involve a contradiction is in that realm of the possible with respect to which God is called omnipotent. Whatever involves a contradiction is not held by omnipotence, for it just cannot possibly make sense of being possible."[18] Continuing his argument with respect to changing the past, Aquinas wrote, "As we have seen, anything that implies a contradiction does not fall under God's omnipotence. For the past not to have been implies a contradiction; thus to say that Socrates is and is not seated is contradictory, and so also to say that he had and had not been seated. To affirm that he had been seated is to affirm a past

---

18   Aquinas: Summa Theologica, Vol. 5, pp. 163-165.

fact, to affirm that he had not been is to affirm what was not the case. Hence for the past not to have been does not lie under divine power. This is what Augustine says, 'Whoever declares that if God is all-powerful let him make the things that have been done not to have been done is making things that are true because they are true also to be false.' And Aristotle speaks to the same effect: 'This alone is lacking in God, the power to make undone the things that once have been done."[19] On the basis of this discussion, there would be good reasons for thinking that petitionary prayers to change the past are of no avail because they ask God to do what cannot be done.

To take a concrete case, after God inflicted Job with innumerable calamities, Job in his suffering said: "Let the day perish wherein I was born, and the night wherein it was said, 'A man-child is brought forth'."[20] By this prayer Job protested against the suffering that had befallen him and expressed the wish that he had never been born. If we assume that Job actually requested that God change the past so that he had not been born, then Job would be asking God to bring about a state of affairs in which two contradictory propositions would be both true. The first proposition is that "Job was born." Clearly, Job would have to have been born for him to utter his prayer. The second proposition "Job was not born" (which is the contradiction of the first) would also have to be true if God granted Job's wish. But since it is impossible for Job both to have been and not to have been born, and since it is likely that God can only do what is logically possible, his prayer could have had no effect as would be the case with all supplications for God to change the past.

---

19   Ibid. pp. 167-169.

20   Job 3:3.

CHAPTER 10

THE PROBLEM OF EVIL AND PETITIONARY PRAYERS

As we have seen, many petitionary prayers seek to rid moral and physical evil from the world. For example the psalmist asked God to deliver him from oppressors and enemies,[1] and Rabbi prayed: "May it be Thy will, O Lord our God, and God of our fathers, to deliver us from the impudent and from impudence, from an evil man, from evil happenings, from the evil impulse, from an evil companion, from an evil neighbour...."[2] It is difficult to understand why God constructed a very cumbersome process by which suffering, pain, injustice, and the like can only be eradicated by means of prayer. If God is all-good as Jews maintain, it does seem it would have been much simpler and more consonant with His nature if He had removed these evils in the first place. Of course if He had done this, there would be no need for these prayers. But since God did not create such a world, we are faced with the dilemma of conceiving how there could be evil in the universe if God is all-good. Thus we can see that the problem of evil is intimately connected with petitionary prayer.

This theological dilemma arises from the fact that evil in both moral and physical terms is an essential element in the universe. But it should be borne in mind that the problem of evil does not arise in connection with every concept of God. It arises, as Hick notes, "only for a religion which insists that the object of its worship is at once perfectly good and unlimitedly powerful."[3] For example in the Greek religion where the gods were viewed as limited in both goodness and power, there would be no inconsistency in asserting that the gods were responsible for the suffering which befell mankind. But if we believe that

---

1   Psalm 17:9; 59:2.

2   Berakoth 16b.

3   J. Hick: <u>Evil and the God of Love</u>, New York, Harper & Row, 1966, p. 4.

there is only one God in the universe who is both all-good and
omnipotent, then there seems to be an inconsistency in believing
that such a God could be responsible for evil.   This problem was
formulated succinctly by Hume: "Is [God] willing to prevent evil,
but not able? then he is impotent.   Is he able, but not willing
then he is malevolent.   Is he both able and willing? whence
then is evil?"[4]   In the words of J. Mackie, this religious
dilemma is "a logical problem, the problem of clarifying and
reconciling a number of beliefs.   In its simplest form the
problem is this: God is omnipotent; God is wholly good; and yet
evil exists.   There seems to be some contradiction between these
three propositions, so that if any two of them were true the
third would be false."[5]

One way of trying to resolve this issue would be to deny
one of the three propositions.   Let us begin with the statement:
"God is omnipotent, and wholly good, but evil does not exist."
It could be argued that evil is an illusion.   On such a view evil
is nothing more than a deprivation of good and thereby has no
being itself.   "For what is that which we call evil but the
absence of good?" St. Augustine asked.   "In the bodies of
animals, disease and wounds mean nothing but the absence of
health; for when a cure is effected, that does not mean that the
evils which were present -namely, the diseases and wounds - go
away from the body and dwell elsewhere: they altogether cease
to exist; for the wound or disease is not a substance, but a
defect in the fleshy substance - the flesh itself being a
substance, and therefore something good of which those evils-
that is, privations of the good which we call health - are

---

4   D. Hume: _Dialogues Concerning Natural Religion_, p. 66.

5   N. Pike (Ed.): _God and Evil_, Englewood Cliffs, New
Jersey, Prentice-Hall, 1964, p. 47. See also E. Stump, _op.cit._

accidents."[6]   By defining evil as a deprivation of good (privatio boni), Augustine tried to demonstrate how apparent evil could exist in a universe created by a wholly good and omnipotent God.   Since evil does not in fact exist (but is rather a deprivation of good), it would be incorrect to assume that God is responsible for its occurrence.   God is only responsible for good, he argued, whether it is present in a large or small degree.   For him evil "is nothing but the corruption of natural measure, form or order.   What is called an evil nature is a corrupt nature.   If it were not corrupt it would be good.   But when it is corrupted, so far as it remains a natural thing, it is good.   It is bad only so far as it is corrupted."[7]   Thus everything that exists is good, and those things which are now less good or no longer good at all have merely fallen away from their original state and have forfeited a part or all of the worth with which they were originally endowed by God.

What Augustine has done by defining evil as a deprivation of good has been to recommend a way of using the word "evil." Such a recommendation would be no more than a semantic preference.   This is Hick's point when he writes, "In the case of any pair of opposite terms, such as large-small, hot-cold, fast-slow, good-evil, it is possible to eliminate one by defining it in terms of the other.   One could for example abolish the word 'small,' and, instead of describing objects as larger and smaller, speak of them instead as being more or less large....   Similarly, one could eliminate the word 'evil' and speak of greater and lesser degrees of goodness.   On such an interpretation Augustine would not be offering an analysis of the actual nature of evil, but would rather be recommending an optimistic vocabulary, and

---

[6]   Augustine: Works IX, Edinburgh, T. & T. Clark, 1873, pp. 181-182.

[7]   J. Hick: Evil and the God of Love, p. 54.

with it an optimistic way of thinking about the world."[8]   Thus we can see that Augustine has not actually succeeded in showing that evil does not exist; he has merely offered a linguistic substitution.

It seems that such an attempt to demonstrate that evil does not exist is doomed to failure.   Evil in both its moral and physical manifestations is a constant and pervasive element in our daily lives.   We have all experienced pain and suffering to some degree, and we cannot help but be aware that the evils of cruelty, savagery, oppression, violence, war as well as catastrophes caused by natural disasters such as floods, earthquakes, fires, and so forth are obtrusive elements in human life.   In Principles of Natural Theology, G.M. Joyce makes this point when he writes, "Disease and death are the lot to which we must all look forward.   At all times, too great numbers of the race are pinched by want.   Nor is the world ever free for very long from the terrible sufferings which follow in the track of war.   If we concentrate our attention on human woes, to the exclusion of the joys of life, we gain an appalling picture of the ills to which the flesh is heir."[9]   Jewish petitionary prayers explicitly recognize the self-evident fact that evil constantly plagues mankind and the Jews in particular; we repeatedly find references to the evils of oppression, immorality, disease, and suffering throughout the Bible, Rabbinic literature, and the Jewish Prayer Book.   It makes no sense to think (as St. Augustine and others have done) that we can remove the problem of evil by denying that evils such as these exist.   The simple fact is that evil is consciously recognized in petitionary prayers and is also an unavoidable element in daily life.   Evil does exist, and we must face the question why God has allowed

---

8   Ibid. p. 60.

9   Pike (Ed.): God and Evil, p. 34.

it, and why He has constructed a process by which it can be eliminated through prayer.

Let us look at the second combination of the three propositions: "God is omnipotent, but not wholly good, and evil does exist." On the basis of this combination, the existence of evil would not pose a theological problem since there would be no inconsistency in believing that a God who was not entirely good could be responsible for evil. Such a God would in some respects be similar to the Greek gods who were likewise not all-good and who occasionally caused suffering and pain. But such a god could not be the God of traditional Judaism. This is not the only consequence of denying the proposition that God is all-good. If the problem of evil is to be solved in this way, the evil which exists must be a direct or an indirect consequence of God's will, and God would have to be very evil indeed. We can see then that if we deny the proposition that God is all-good in attempting to solve the problem of evil, we are left with a God who (unlike God as described in Jewish sources) is basically immoral. And of course if God is like this, it is fruitless to pray to Him. God might grant such prayers, but there would be no assurance that He would. Indeed such petitionary prayers might in fact be opposed to God's intentions. This would of course be an explanation why petitionary prayers for God to perform moral actions (such as healing the sick) often go unanswered. But such an explanation could only be formulated at the expense of God's attributes. And if God does not have the nature that has been traditionally ascribed to Him, it is difficult to conceive how he could be worthy of being worshipped. He might be feared, and one might offer prayers of praise and adoration in order to coerce Him not to act in wicked fashion. But this would be a very different incentive from the type of heartfelt worship as we find in Psalm 42:1, "As the heart panteth after the water-brooks, so panteth my soul after Thee, O God."

The third combination of the three propositions: "God is not omnipotent, but He is wholly good, and evil does exist," suggests that God is not the cause of moral and physical evil in the world - since God is limited in power He is not able to prevent such evil.   There is no contradiction in believing that God is wholly good and that evil exists.   He would prevent such evil if He could, but as He is limited in power He is unable to do so.   Such an account of the origin of evil due to God's limitation suffers from serious weaknesses.   If God is not able to prevent evil, it is difficult to understand why He created the universe in the first place.   Surely He would have known that His creation would be subject to physical catastrophes which would cause great suffering, and that human beings would act immorally toward one another.   If God is wholly good, it is unclear why He would have created all that exists, knowing that He would not be able to control or eliminate such evils.   And even if there were more good than evil in the universe, this would not explain why God created a world in which He knew that there would be such a large quantity of physical and moral evil.   Another difficulty with this explanation is that it presupposes that God is extremely limited in power.   In order to preserve the truth of the proposition "God is wholly good," we have to conclude that God is very limited in what He can do- a very unpalatable conclusion in light of Biblical and rabbinic teaching about God's nature.   Furthermore if God is unable to eliminate evils which plague mankind, it does seem fruitless to offer petitionary prayers to Him to do just this.   Since there is so much evil in the universe which God has not removed, there seems to be no justification for believing that He would be able to grant prayers.

In the preceding discussion I tried to show that if one denies any of the three propositions about God's nature and the existence of evil, one is met by very serious problems.   It may be that another theological approach is possible.   One explanation for the existence of human suffering is that good cannot exist without evil - therefore God has created evil as a necessary counterpart to good. Such a solution imples that there is a limit to what God can do; saying that good cannot exist without evil suggests that God cannot create good without simultaneously creating its opposite. A parallel argument is that God occasionally uses evil as a means to good. On this account one could conclude that God allowed the destruction of six million Jews in the last World War in order for the state of Israel to come into existence. But such explanations again presuppose a severe restriction of God's potency. If God is all-powerful there is no reason to think that He would be restricted in such a fashion.

Another explanation why evil exists is that the universe is better with some evil in it than it would be if there were none. Such an argument could mean that in an aesthetic sense evil contrasts with good in such a way as to create a more pleasing harmony. In the words of Mackie, "the best organization of the universe will not be static, but progressive, that the gradual overcoming of evil by good is really a finer thing than would be the eternal unchallenged supremacy of good."[10]   Yet this explanation also fails because it overlooks the fact that pain, suffering, misery, death, and so forth are exceedingly unpleasant aspects of daily life. It could be objected that this argument merely asserts that the world would be a better place if there were some evil in it; it does not assert that the world would be a better place if all evil were retained. Evil sometimes serves a beneficial physical and moral purpose. For example, we read in a standard medical textbook that pain serves important protective functions; "In the first place, pain serves as a means of alarm.... It is the symptom of all others which induces a patient to seek the expert advice of a physician or surgeon....

---

[10]   Pike (Ed.): God and Evil, p. 53.

In the second place, pain acts as an invaluable deterrent...."[11] With regard to the morally beneficial results of evil, Joyce writes that "one reason plainly why God permits suffering is that man may rise to a height of heroism which would otherwise have been beyond his scope. Nor are these the only benefits which it confers. That sympathy for others which is one of the most precious parts of our experience, and one of the most fruitful sources of well-doing, has its origin in the fellow-feeling engendered by endurance of similar trials."[12] Surely pain can serve a beneficial function, but this does not mean that the world is better as a result. Such an argument merely begs the question because if evil in all its manifestations were removed from the universe, there would be no reason for pain to alert humans to serious physical problems nor for men to suffer in order to feel empathy for other human beings.

What are we to say about the argument that evil is a necessary by-product of the laws of the universe which produce beneficial results. This is the sort of argument Leibniz used when he proclaimed that ours is "the best of all possible worlds." "The wisdom of God," he wrote "not content with embracing all the possibles, penetrates them, compares them, weighs them one against the other, to estimate their degrees of perfection or imperfection, the strong and the weak, the good and the evil.... By this means the divine Wisdom distributes all the possibles it had already contemplated separately, into so many universal systems which it further compares the one with the other. The result of all these comparisons and deliberations is the choice of the best from among all these possible

---

11   H. Balme: The Relief of Pain: A Handbook of Modern Analgesia, London, J.A. Churchill, Ltd., 1939, pp. 5-6.

12   Pike (Ed.): God and Evil, p. 73.

systems."[13]   According to Leibniz, evil is a necessary ingredient in this "best of all possible worlds." "All the evils of the world contribute," he wrote "... to the character of the whole as the best of all possible universes... if the smallest evil that comes to pass in the world were missing in it, it would no longer be this world."[14]   Unfortunately Leibniz did not defend this assertion. "I cannot show you this in detail," he wrote "nor can I present infinities to you and compare them together.   But you must judge with me *ab effectu,* since God has chosen this world as it is."[15]   Thus Leibniz's confidence that our world is the best of all possible worlds is based on his faith that our world has been created by an all-powerful and wholly good God; it would have been inconsistent with His nature to have created anything else. If our world had such a character, it would be the best of all possible worlds.   But it is not.   Surely our world would be better if such evils as disease, war, human suffering, violence and oppression were eliminated.   Perhaps what Leibniz meant is that it would have been impossible for God to make a better world than the one He did make - not because our world is the best imaginable, but because God was powerless to make a better one.   But if God is able to do anything, there is no reason why God's power should be limited in this way.

Another explanation for the existence of evil is that it is due to human free will.   According to this argument, God chose to give men free choice so that they would be able to attain higher goods than would be possible otherwise.   In this connection, Flew writes, "this precious yet dangerous 'gift of free will' necessarily implies, not only the possibility of choosing what is good, but also the possibility of choosing what

---

[13]   G. Leibniz: Theodicy, London, Routledge & Kegan Paul, Ltd., 1952, para. 225.

[14]   Ibid. para 9.

[15]   Ibid. para. 10.

is bad; that the unfortunate, altogether familiar fact is that some, perhaps most, of God's creatures usually - although the choice and hence the fault is, of course, always theirs and not his - pick wrong rather than right options; but that, nevertheless all the evil of and consequent upon all these wrong choices by creatures is in the end more than offset by the actually achieved sum of those higher goods of which the capacity to choose is the logically necessary condition."[16]

This defence of free will is mistaken for a number of reasons. First, there are evils in the world which are not traceable back to human wickedness. One needs only to look at countless examples of physical catastrophes such as floods, earthquakes, fires, hurricanes, as well as the fact that mankind is plagued by diseases (such as cancer and Aids) to see that a very large portion of human suffering is not caused by man himself. This solution also suffers from the assumption that it is better that men should act freely, and sometimes err, than that their behaviour should be predetermined. It is inconceivable that virtues obtained by acting freely (such as heroism, courage and piety) are more important than the suffering that mankind endures through immoral actions which are committed because men have free will. This is not to underestimate such virtues; they are valuable and can be obtained only because men are able to act freely rather than under compulsion. But these virtues (though valuable in themselves) seem of little significance in relation to the enormous amount of pain that humanity is forced to endure. For instance, there seems no comparison between the heroism that soldiers can freely attain in war and the suffering that war brings. If one were given the choice between eliminating war or denying human beings the possibility to become heroes by predetermining that they would never engage in war, there

---

16   A. Flew: "Compatibilism, Free Will and God," Philosophy, 1973, p. 232.

seems little question what the choice would be. Thus if God is wholly good as the Jewish tradition maintains, it seems more consonant with His goodness that He would have chosen to prevent human suffering by predetermining that men only did what was right rather than give them free will so that they would act cruelly and immorally. The alternative is, as H. McCloskey wrote, "on the one hand, rational agents with free wills making many bad and some good decisions on rational and nonrational grounds, and 'rational' agents predestined always to 'choose' the right things for the right reasons.... God were He omnipotent, could preordain the decisions and the reasons upon which they were based; and such a mode of existence would seem in itself a worthy mode of existence, and one preferable to an existence with free will, irrationality, and evil."[17]

Another explanation for the existence of evil is that it is God's punishment for sin. This explanation is found in numerous passages in the Bible as well as throughout Jewish sources. In the book of Job, for example, Eliphaz the Temanite expressed this view when he pointed out to Job that his sufferings could only be the consequence of wrongdoing. "This I know," he asserted "that those who plough mischief and sow trouble reap as they have sown; they perish at the blast of God and are shrivelled by the breath of his nostrils."[18] But it is not only the wicked who suffer - those who are righteous or innocent equally share misfortune and sorrow. The fact that children who are in no way responsible for their actions are born deformed or suffer and die during the first few years of their lives are obvious counter-examples to this claim. In the words of McCloskey, "no crime or sin of the child can explain and justify these physical evils as punishment; and, for a

---

17   Pike (Ed.): <u>God and Evil</u>, p. 83.

18   Job 4:8-9.

parent's sin to be punished in the child is injustice or evil of another kind."[19]

It might be argued that God tests people through suffering (as He did in the case of Job) in order to demonstrate that they will remain firm despite their suffering, and thereby act as a salutary example to others. Such an argument however overlooks the fact that not everyone who suffers is able to remain pious - there are many examples of individuals who simply renounce God. Moreover it is difficult to understand how God could be wholly good if He causes persons to suffer merely as a test. Furthermore, such an explanation would not account for evils such as mass disasters and catastrophes which result in the loss of human lives; in such cases, it would be impossible for those who died to serve as examples. A final explanation for the existence of evil is that God causes natural catastrophes such as earthquakes, floods, and the like in order to demonstrate His power so that men will have the proper reverence for Him and keep His commandments. The problem with this view is that it does not account for the existence of moral evils (such as oppression and justice). In the words of McCloskey, it "is hardly the course one would expect of a benevolent God to adopt when other, more effective, less evil methods are available to Him, for example, miracles, special revelations, etc."[20]

In this chapter, we have uncovered a seemingly unanswerable problem; even supposing that prayer does eradicate evil, how can we believe that an all-good and all-powerful God has permitted such evils to exist and constructed a process by which petitionary prayers can eliminate them? If we assume that God is not all-good, or not all-powerful in an attempt to solve the problem of evil, our difficulties increase. If evil is

---

19   Pike (Ed.): God and Evil, p. 69.

20   Ibid. p. 69.

really an illusion, then there is no point in praying for its eradication since it does not exist anyway. If God is not really all-good but all-powerful, there is no point in praying for the eradication of evil since God clearly does not want to eradicate it. But if God is not really all-powerful but all-good, there seems to be no point in praying since God simply cannot eradicate evil even if He wanted to. "

CHAPTER 11

OMNISCIENCE, OMNIPOTENCE, UNCHANGEABLENESS AND PETITIONARY PRAYERS

In the last chapter I discussed the difficulty of reconciling the belief that petitionary prayers are sometimes efficacious in eliminating evil with the view that God is all-good and all-powerful. In this chapter we will consider whether the attributes of omniscience, omnipotence, and unchangeableness conflict with the presuppositions of petitionary prayer. If God is omniscient, presumably He would know the future since by definition He knows everything. According to Aquinas, "God knows all things, not only those which exist in actuality, but those which are in the potency of himself or of a creature, and some of these are contingent events in our future, it follows that God knows contingent future events... future contingents cannot be certain to us, because we know them as future contingents; they can be certainly only to God, whose act of knowledge is in eternity, above time."[1]

Some writers have disputed this understanding of omniscience; they claim that God can be omniscient without knowing future events. In "The Formalities of Omniscience," A. Prior argues that Aquinas was wrong in thinking that God's knowledge is above time: "Many very reputable philosophers, eg. St. Thomas Aquinas have held that God's knowledge is in some way right outside of time.... I want to argue against this view, on the grounds that its final effect is to restrict what God knows to those truths, if any, which are themselves timeless. For example, God could not, on the view I am considering, know that the 1970 final examinations at Manchester are now over; for this isn't something that He or anyone could know timelessly, because it just isn't true timelessly. It's true now,

---

1   Aquinas: Summa Theologica, vol. 4, pp. 47-51.

but it wasn't true a year ago."[2]   Prior's point is that God can
only know at a certain point in time what is true then.   In
other words, at a particular point in time (T_1), God can know
only what is true at T_1.   If a proposition is not true at T_1,
then God could not know it to be true then.   Furthermore,
Prior argues that with respect to a voluntary action occurring in
the future relative to a given time (T_2), the claim that this
action will be performed at T_2 is not true at T_1.   This is so
because the claim that the action will be performed at T_2 is
neither true nor false at T_1.   In God and Timelessness, N. Pike
explains Prior's position as follows: "It follows, Prior says, that
an omniscient being existing at T_1 could not know at T_1 that a
voluntary action of a certain description will be performed at
T_2. God does not have foreknowledge of human actions."[3]

Let us assume, for example, that my aunt took a trip to
Paris last Sunday.   If it is true (as Aquinas asserts), that God
knows all future events, then eighty years ago God would have
known that this event would take place.   My aunt could
therefore not have done otherwise - to suppose that she would
be able to refrain from making this trip would be to render
false a proposition which was true eighty years earlier.   For
God to have knowledge of future human actions and events (like
my aunt taking a trip to Paris last Sunday), it must be the case
that propositions describing human actions are true at times
prior to the times that the events take place.   But, as Prior
argues, the fact that a man acts in a certain way is not
knowable prior to the time the action occurs.   Thus he writes:
"I can by my free choice, not exercised until tomorrow, cause a

---

2   A. Prior: Times and Tense, Oxford Clarendon Press,
1968, p. 29.   See also B. Hebblethwaite: 'Some Reflections on
Predestination, Providence and Divine Foreknowledge,' Religious
Studies, 15, 1979.

3   N. Pike: God and Timelessness, London, Routledge &
Kegan Paul, 1970, p. 65.

person's guess, made yesterday, to have been a correct one (I do this simply by deciding to do what he guessed I would).... But while contingent futures, and contingent future-inflicted pasts, can in this way be correctly or incorrectly guessed, I cannot see in what way they can be 'known'; or to put it another way, I cannot see in what way the alleged knowledge, even if it were God's, could be more than correct guessing."[4]

According to Prior, God could not know at T_1 an event would take place at T_2, because God would lack sufficient grounds for having such knowledge. God might make a correct guess, but He could never have knowledge of what was going to happen. It would only be after an event had taken place or while an event was taking place that God could have knowledge of it. It is for this reason that he writes "There would be ex hypothesi nothing that could make it (God's guessing about future events) knowledge, no present ground for the guess's correctness, which a specially penetrating person might perceive.... God could not possibly have any knowledge of future contingencies if He knows them as future... as He knows them, they are not still to come, but already there."[5]

Other writers have disputed this view. According to N. Pike, Prior is wrong in thinking that future events cannot be known. "What reason," Pike asks "is there for supposing that this is the only way that God could know what will happen in the future?" God, Pike argues, could be compared in terms of His knowledge of the future to a crystal-ball gazer. In this way, Pike believes, God's foreknowledge would not be the outcome of a prediction based on evidence. It would be the result of a 'vision' involving nothing in the way of an inference

---

4   Ibid. p. 36.

5   Ibid. pp. 36-38.

or calculation.[6]   There would be no reason, Pike asserts, "for insisting that 'Jones does A at T_2' must be true at T_1 if God is to know at T_1 that Jones does A at T_2. To insist on this would be to disregard the special 'visionary' nature of God's foreknowledge."[7]

Pike is wrong, however, in thinking that he resolves this dilemma. Regardless of whether God predicts the future on the basis of evidence or whether He knows the future like a "visionary," if God knows what will happen in the future what He knows is true. In other words, Prior is right in insisting that the proposition "x does such and such an act at T_2" must be true at T_1 if God is to know at T_1 that x does such and such an act at T_2. Whether this knowledge is derived from evidence or through a visionary process is irrelevant. Prior's analysis rests on the idea that God lives in time. Because Prior's God experiences time as we do (remembering the past, experiencing the present, and looking forward to the future), He can have no real knowledge of the future; He can only make a well-informed guess. This, according to Prior, does not prevent Him from being omniscient (defined as the ability to know everything it is possible to know at the present time). For example, at this moment God knows there were dinosaurs on the earth millions of years ago. He can remember a time when the proposition "there are dinosaurs on the earth" was true. But if dinosaurs return to the earth a million years hence, when this actually happens (thereby making the proposition "There are dinosaurs on the earth" again true), then God will know about it. However because He lives in time, He will not know about it until it actually happens: God may be able to make an

---

6   Pike: God and Timelessness, pp. 64-65.

7   Ibid. p. 69.

informed guess since He has seen the advent of dinosaurs before, but He cannot know it for certain.

Despite the attractive implications for prayer of Prior's theory, it does not conform to the traditional Jewish picture of God. Traditionally God is outside time. He does not live in the present, have a past or look forward to the future; He lives in the eternal Now. This is very hard for human beings to understand since it is totally outside the sphere of our experience. It is only possible to catch a glimpse before the curtain of incomprehension comes down. The idea is that God is experiencing every moment in the past and future history of the created world simultaneously and eternally. What for us are fleeting moments rushing by, bring one experience after another, are a huge static tapestry for God of which He sees every part continually. The nearest analogy perhaps is that of a cinema film. When we go to the cinema, we see shown on the screen the experiences of other people. Almost invariable they are portrayed in the order in which they occurred. But if after the film, instead of stumbling out of the cinema to continue the course of our own lives, we go into the room where the film was projected, we will be able to look at the film roll itself. We would discover that it is a series of little pictures, and when we look at it, we can perhaps have some experience of God's timelessness. We see all these little pictures simultaneously which we had previously experienced in a temporal sequence. Of course as we are not all-powerful, we cannot look in detail at more than one picture at a time, but nonetheless we are experiencing something of the supposed timelessness of God.

If we accept this picture of God, we must accept that He knows the future since after all he is already experiencing it. God's timeless knowledge is knowledge of everything which is true - past, present and future. Putting this in a slightly more formalized language than colloquial English, we could say (where p symbolizes any statement): "For all p, if it is the case that p, God has always known that it would be the case that p." Such a formula would cover past-tensed instantiations like the following: "If there were dinosaurs on earth millions of years ago, then God knows that there were dinosaurs on earth millions of years ago." Similarly future-tensed instantiations like the following would also be covered: "If there will be living organisms a million years hence, then God knows that there will be living organisms a million years hence."[8]

If God's knowledge is like this, it is difficult to understand how prayers for God to affect the future would be efficacious. If God knows for example that my aunt is not going to recover from her illness, then this is what is going to happen. I might as well give up praying for her recovery. Because God can see now and has always seen that she will not recover, nothing can change that fact. My prayer would be of no avail. We can also see that if God is experiencing the future now, there can be no voluntary human actions. This would be so since no person would be able to act in such a way as to alter events in his life which God at a prior point in time would have known would take place in the future. What we can see then is that there is a clash here between the belief that God is omniscient and the belief that human actions can be voluntary. In The City of God, St. Augustine formulated the dilemma thus: "If all things have been foreknown; and if they came to pass in this order, there is a certain order of causes, for nothing can happen which is not preceded by some efficient cause. But if there is a certain order of causes according to which everything happens which does happen, then by fate... all things happen which happen. But if this be so, then there is nothing in our own power and there is no such thing as freedom of will; and if we

---

8   Prior: Time and Tense, p. 25.

grant this... the whole economy of human life is subverted."[9]   In other words, if I am trying to make up my mind whether or not to join the Mafia, at this very moment God is experiencing my first bloody massacre.   Consequently, the moral dilemma I am going through is really of no avail since I am going to join anyway.   I may go through real moral anguish in making my decision; God sees this, but He still knows which way I am going to go.   The freedom of choice which I believe I experience is an illusion.   Furthermore if human actions are involuntary and men are not responsible for their actions, it makes no sense to ask God for forgiveness for sin - the notion of sin would vanish if it were not the result of a voluntary choice.

Although this seems an inescapable conclusion, there is one way out of the dilemma.   This is a very tentative solution, and one which may be merely an apologist's attempt to have it both ways.   It may be that when we make a moral choice, we are doing something real within the <u>context of time</u>.   When I try to decide whether to join the Mafia, God knows what my decision will be not because He has foreknowledge but because the future as well as the present is Now for Him.   But for me the future is the future, and in the context of the present, I am making a real moral choice; I really could at the present time decide not to join the Mafia.   God does not know the future because we are God-directed robots; we are not like actors in a film whose moves are planned by the director.   Rather we are free beings; because I make a free choice to join the Mafia, God experiences my first crime.   If I had not decided to join, God would have experienced something else.   His experience is dependent on our choices.   Because He lives outside time, He happens to experience all these things simultaneously,   but the fact that He

_____

9   Pike: <u>God and Timelessness</u>, pp. 64-65.

experiences all time simultaneously does not necessarily mean that His experience is not dependent on our choices.

If it is the case that human moral decisions are real moral decisions (although God knows the future) what are the consequences for petitionary prayer? Is it possible that God both knows the future and that petitionary prayers could make a difference? Suppose my aunt is very ill in hospital, and let us say that I pray for her and she recovers. When I prayed for her, I did not know she was going to recover, but God did. At the moment of receiving my prayer He was experiencing her recovery. But even though I was making a real moral choice when I chose to say a prayer, it is difficult to see that prayer would make any real difference to the state of my relative's health. Perhaps if I prayed for strength to look after her if she recovered, this might have some psychological effect on me, since making such a prayer is much the same thing as making a moral decision at the present time to look after her. But when I pray for someone else, my prayer is not a present moral decision. It refers to the future. Therefore if God is already experiencing the future, it is difficult to understand how it could be altered by prayer. A believer might argue however that in the same way God's experience is dependent on man's choices, so His experience is also dependent on man's prayers. In other words, if I had not prayed for my aunt's recovery because I had not chosen to do so, then God would not have experienced her recovery. Perhaps this is the case; if it is so, it is extremely difficult to understand, but it means one could believe both that God is omniscient in the traditional sense and that petitionary prayer is a worthwhile exercise.

To sum up, if we accept the traditional interpretation of God's omniscience, we have two alternatives. We can say that as God is outside time and life is like a reel of film. God looks at all the pictures on the reel of film simultaneously and eternally. We however are like the actors in the film: we experience life from one moment to the next. As God knows what all the pictures are on the film, we have no real choice but to play our foreordained roles. We are like marionettes in a puppet show. If God is omniscient and if He knows the future, then we can only conclude that petitionary prayers for Him to change the future could not possibly be efficacious, and that is the end of the matter. However it may be that there is no good human analogy for God's timeless relationship with the world and man. Life could be seen as a reel of film. God can see all the pictures on the film simultaneously and eternally, but then the analogy breaks down. We are not like film actors on a set with a zealous director. Instead the final film which God experiences then, now and always, is dependent on the free moral decisions of human beings. Of course God knows what those decisions are since He is already experiencing their effects, but in the context of the present they are real moral decisions. If this view is correct, petitionary prayer does not necessarily become a meaningful activity, but it is not completely hopeless as it is according to the first view. This latter explanation goes against any of our preconceived logical categories. If it is the case that God's "film reel" is dependent on human prayers, we cannot explain how this is so; we can only assert it.

Let us now turn to the notion that God is all-powerful (or omnipotent). In Chapter 2 I discussed the idea of God doing impossible things, and we saw that some philosophers maintain that even though God is omnipotent, there are certain actions which He cannot perform. They do not consider that God could change the past. In recent literature some modern philosophers extend this argument and assert that there are some things God cannot do even though those things are not impossible by definition. For example, as Swinburne points out, "getting married" is an action that can be performed only by a married person, "committing adultery with an unmarried man is an action that can be performed only by a married woman... sitting down can only be done by an embodied being, becoming incarnate can only be done by a disembodied being, etc."[10]   Thus, divine omnipotence should be regarded not simply as an ability to do any logically possible action, but as an ability to perform any action of a kind which is logically possible for God.   Such a definition conforms to Maimonides' contention that "it is impossible that God should produce a being like Himself, or annihilate, corporify, or change Himself...."[11]

Yet, regardless of the way in which one defines the concept of divine omnipotence, all definitions describe what God can do; no definition asserts that God does in fact perform all those actions which He can perform.   This point was brought out by Aquinas when he wrote, "when you say that God has the power for everything, you are most correctly interpreted as meaning this: that since power is relative to what is possible, divine power can do everything that is possible, and on this account is God called omnipotent."[12]   For Aquinas God could do anything which is logically possible; it was not his intention to assert that everything that has occurred, or everything which will happen is the result of God's will.   Since these definitions do not presuppose that every event which has happened or will happen is the result of God's will, there is no reason to assume that because God is omnipotent, petitionary prayers would be of no avail.   Thus, if it is the case that God can perform any action which is logically possible, it does not follow that petitionary prayers for God to bring about future events are of no avail; if the requests were for God to perform actions which

---

10   R.   Swinburne: "Omnipotence,"   American   Philosophical Quarterly, July, 1973.

11   Maimonides: The Guide of the Perplexed, Part III, pp. 59-61.

12   Aquinas: Summa Theologica, Vol. 5, p. 163.

are logically possible, they could be efficacious. Since God is able to affect the future course of events, there would be no reason to assume that He would not grant the petitions made to Him particularly if they were made for worthy ends.

Even though these definitions of God's omnipotence do not presuppose that all events which have occurred and will occur are the product of God's will, it has been maintained throughout Jewish religious literature that God's will has been the cause of creation as well as innumerable events in the life of the Jews. We read in Genesis, that God created heaven and earth,[13] light,[14] seas,[15] grass,[16] planets and stars,[17] living creatures,[18] man and woman.[19] In Exodus, we read that God caused the Red Sea to divide,[20] and manna to descend from heaven.[21] In Rabbinic literature as well as the Jewish Prayer Book, we also read that God caused and continually causes events to occur. For example, we read in the eighteen benedictions of the evening service for Hanukkah: "We thank thee for the miracles, for the redemption, for the mighty deeds and triumphs, and for the battles which thou didst perform for our fathers in those days.... In every generation we will thank thee and recount thy praise - for our lives which are in thy charge, for our souls

---

13   Gen. 1:1.

14   Gen. 1:3.

15   Gen. 1:10.

16   Gen. 1:12.

17   Gen. 1:14.

18   Gen. 1:20.

19   Gen. 1:27.

20   Ex. 14:21.

21   Ex. 16:14.

which are in thy care, for thy miracles which are daily with us, and for thy continual wonders and favors - evening, morning and noon."[22]   If God has created the universe and is responsible for bringing about so many events, does this mean that petitionary prayers can have no effect on God's will?   There is no reason for this to be so.   The fact that God has been the cause of so many happenings merely demonstrates that God could fulfil the requests which are made to Him in petitionary prayers.   For example the fact that God caused Israel to be victorious in battle does not in any way imply that prayers for God to bring about such events would be of no avail.   On the contrary it shows that God does grant requests.

But what if God is the cause of all events?   It is possible to assume from the overwhelming number of God's interventions that God is responsible for whatsoever comes to pass.   Such a view would make God, in the words of Flew, "a quasi-personal being (who) has fixed everything that everyone will do, and choose, and suffer."[23]   Thus the whole course of events would be under God's control and would include every human thought and action as well as every natural event.   Does such a view imply that petitionary prayers are of no avail?   This seems to be Flew's conclusion in "Divine Omnipotence and Human Freedom."   Here he writes that this view is a form of predestination, and he argues that according to predestination "all of us are, really and ultimately, as it were acting out the irresistible suggestions of the Great Hypnotist (God)...   Now, certainly," he continues, "if we were to discover that a person or group of people, whom previously we had thought to be acting freely and therefore to be properly accountable in law and morals for what they misdid, had in fact been acting out

---

22   Daily Prayer Book, p. 208.

23   A Flew: New Essays in Philosophical Theology, London, SCM Press, 1955.

the suggestions of some master-hypnotist, then we should need to reconsider all questions of their accountability in the light of this fresh information."[24]   The implication of Flew's explanation is that since no person is able to act freely, petitionary prayers are of no avail since all events including the making of prayers are predetermined by God.

But Flew is wrong about this.   He is correct in assuming that since God is the cause of everything, "it would be monstrous to suggest that anyone, however truly responsible in the eyes of men, could fairly be called to account and punished by the God who had rigged his every move."[25]   In other words, if all human action is the result of God's will, it would be mistaken to assume that human beings could be held responsible for their actions.   But Flew is wrong in thinking that if God is the cause of everything which occurs, this implies that all events are predetermined.   It is possible for God to be the cause of an event without actually planning for it to take place. Such a situation often occurs in our daily lives.   I might for example accidentally cause a car accident, thereby injuring both myself and the other driver.   But the fact that I would be the cause does not imply that I planned for the accident to take place.   Similarly in the case of those events which God allegedly brings about, there is no reason to assume that they are the result of divine predestination.   It is conceivable that God could bring about occurrences (such as the parting of the Red Sea) without having planned it at an earlier stage.   Divine omnipotence, even if it is interpreted as God's power in bringing about whatever happens, should be sharply distinguished from divine omniscience.   If God does not plan what events will occur prior to their occurrence, petitionary prayers could be of avail.

---

24   Ibid. p. 162.

25   Ibid. p. 163.

There are nevertheless prayers which it would be illogical to make given this view of omnipotence. If God is responsible for causing all actions, there is no point in praying "forgive us our trespasses" since God - being the cause of these actions - is also responsible for them. Jews, however, do not believe that God is just omnipotent; they want to insist on His omniscience as well. Despite this it is quite possible to imagine a God who is omnipotent without being omniscient. For example, it is possible to imagine a God who answers my prayers for my aunt's recovery, but who does not know that because of this recovery my aunt would have a perfectly miserable remainder to her life, emotionally crippled with hypochondria which she developed because she so missed people fussing round her. It would be easy to understand how this kind of God allows evil in the world - He simply does not know about it. If God is like this, there is a point to petitionary prayer. But Jews insist that God is omniscient as well as omnipotent.

What are we to say about the belief that God is unchanging? Aquinas in the <u>Summa Theologica</u> expressed a major objection to the view that petitionary prayer can change God's will. "By prayer (petitionary prayer)," he wrote, "we bend the mind of the person to whom we pray, so that he may do what is asked of him. But God's mind is unchangeable and inflexible.... Therefore, it is not fitting that we should pray to God."[26] But what does it mean to say that God is unchanging? According to Aquinas "God, being limitless and embracing within himself the whole fullness of perfection of all existence, cannot acquire anything, nor can he move out towards something previously not attained." Clearly if we believe that petitionary prayers affect God in that they cause Him to do something, and if God thereby undergoes change, then petitionary prayers cannot work since God by definition cannot change. The

---

[26]   Aquinas: <u>Summa Theologica</u>, Vol. 39, pp. 50-51.

question is whether fulfilling a petitionary prayer really causes a change in God. What exactly constitutes such a change? It is tempting to assume that whenever God is described as undergoing any alteration such as knowing one thing and then another (willing one thing and then another and so forth), He undergoes change.

One way of approaching this problem is to formulate a precise criterion for determining whether a change has taken place in an object - thus it would be possible to determine whether changing from a state of not willing to a state of willing, or vice versa, would constitute a change in God. One of the most widely-known formulations of such a criterion is the "Cambridge criterion" which was proposed by Russell and MacTaggart. According to these philosophers, an object (x) has changed if we have, for some interpretation of "F," "t" and "t$_1$," the two propositions: (1) "F (x) at time T_1" is true and (2) "F (x) at time T_2" is false. For example, if the following two premises are true: "The flower is blooming at time T_1 is true," and "The flower is blooming at time T_2 is false," then we should conclude that the flower has changed. In the case of God, if the following two premises are true: "God willed to do x at time T_1 is true," and "God willed to do x at time T_2 is false," then it follows accordingly that God has Himself undergone a change.

But is the "Cambridge criterion" an accurate criterion for determining whether an object has undergone change? In God and the Soul, Peter Geach points out that this criterion is intuitively unsatisfactory, because in certain cases it would imply that an object has changed, whereas in fact it had not done so.[27] For example, as Geach notes, if it is the case that "'Socrates is taller than Theaetetus at time T_1' is true," and "'Socrates is taller than Theaetetus at T_2' is false," then it follows, according to the "Cambridge criterion," that Socrates

---

[27]   Geach: God and the Soul, p. 72.

has changed.   But this would be false since the explanation why
Socrates was taller than Theaetetus at time T_1 and not taller at
time T_2 is simply that Theaetetus grew taller than Socrates.
Thus the change would be in Theaetetus, not in Socrates.
Therefore the "Cambridge criterion" is an inadequate criterion
for determining whether an object has changed, and it should
not be used to determine whether God has Himself changed if
He changes from a state of willing to not willing, or vice versa.
Thus Geach writes: "I do not know of any criterion, let alone a
sharp one, that will tell us when we have a real change... and
not just a 'Cambridge' change." [28]   Does this mean that when
God is described as altering in some way, we must conclude that
it is impossible to tell whether God has in fact changed?   In
the case of God's knowledge, where God is described as knowing
one thing at a particular point in time, and a different thing at
a different point in time, such an alteration in God's knowledge
does not indicate that God Himself had undergone a change.
This is the point N. Kretzman makes in "Omniscience and
Immutability" where he argues that a change in an object which
is known does not necessitate a change in the knower.   "For
example," he writes, "I know that the Chrysler Building in
Manhattan is 1,046 feet tall.   If it is said that the Chrysler
Building is the object of my knowledge, then of course many
changes in it - in its tenants or in its heating system, for
example - do not necessitate changes in the state of my
knowledge."[29]

But it could be argued that although changes in the object
which is known do not necessitate a change in the knower, it is
nevertheless the case that if one knows the changing of an

---

[28]   Ibid. p. 99.   For a further discussion of this issue see
V. Brummer, op.cit., pp. 37-40.

[29]   N. Kretzman, "Omniscience and Immutability," The
Journal of Philosophy, July, 1966, p. 411.

object, the knower also undergoes a change. And whoever knows first one proposition and then another undergoes a change. This analysis would hold true in the case of persons who know one thing and then another, but it would not be true in the case of God. If God is omniscient, then God knows every change in the universe all at once rather than successively. Thus it makes no sense to think that because an object changes, God must also undergo change. Since God is omniscient, His knowledge is not like a person's in that, in the words of Aquinas, "God considers all that He knows not successively, but together."[30] Because God knows all changes in the universe simultaneously, then a pair of premises like "It was once true to say: God knows that Socrates is sitting down" and "It is now no longer true to say: God knows that Socrates is sitting down" would not imply that God has changed. In the case of God's knowledge even if we lack a precise criterion for determining whether God has undergone a change, it is logical to assume that when God is described as knowing one thing and then another, this does not imply that He has changed. But what are we to say in the case where God is described as changing from a state of willing to a state of not willing, or vice versa?

In normal life we know exactly what a change is. If on Rosh Hashanah, the rabbi does not get on with the cantor and they never speak to one another, and if at Succot, they seem friendly and never make a decision without consulting one another, then a change has obviously taken place. So it is with all examples of earthly change; the idea of time comes in. Something was the case at one moment in time and ceased to be the case at another moment in time. But God is not in time. Although it may appear from our perspective that in the dialogue with Abraham, God was about to destroy the city of Sodom at one moment and at another moment He was prepared

---

30   Ibid. p. 413.

to save it, if He really is outside time, the believer would have to argue that he was really doing both these things at once, simultaneously and eternally.   If we see God's will as God manifesting His desires in a temporal context, then in the story of Sodom His will underwent a change.   Yet the believer would have to argue that God Himself viewed from His own perspective outside time underwent no change.

What bearing does this have on petitionary prayer?   Let us imagine a university lecturer in theology who very much wants to become Master of his college.   Let us imagine that the Old Master is due to retire and that the theologian has only one serious rival - a physicist.   In his desire to be Master, the theologian might invoke God's help.   Leaving aside the difficulty that it seems rather unfair if God supports him rather than the physicist on account of his expertise in prayer, is it possible that God would give the position to the physicist?   Can God really change His mind like that?   If God is outside time, it is perhaps possible that God thinks that the physicist and the theologian should both have the job.   The believer would certainly have to argue that God wanted both men to be the Master and that He wanted this simultaneously and eternally. But how can this be?   If God changes His mind in time, then in eternity He must will both situations.   There is no escaping this conclusion, and yet it is unbelievable.   God knows that only one person can be the Master and, since the theologian and the physicist are not identical people, one must on balance be more suitable for the post than the other.   God cannot believe that they have equal claims.   How can He will that the theologian be the Master and, at the same time, will that the physicist hold this position?   Yet this is what He must will if He can be persuaded to change His mind in time as the result of prayer. Similarly if God is undecided whom to appoint to the post, and if He makes up His mind as the result of prayer, this also involves a contradiction. God cannot be both decided and undecided simultaneously and eternally.

In this chapter I have discussed whether it is possible to believe in the efficacy of prayer as well as in the traditional Jewish picture of God as omniscient, omnipotent, and unchanging. We have seen that it is just possible to believe in God's omniscience and the efficacy of petitionary prayer, though this involves notions which are very difficult, if not impossible to understand. Yet the simplest and clearest explanation is that because of God's omniscience, petitionary prayers cannot possibly be efficacious. When it comes to omnipotence, however, there is no difficulty in believing that an omnipotent (though not omniscient) God could answer prayer. But it is not possible to believe in the efficacy of prayer if God is changeless. The presupposition behind petitionary prayer is that God can change the course of events as a result of prayer. Yet, if a changeless God who is outside time does this, then He has to will two contradictory states of affairs simultaneously and eternally. This must be impossible.

CONCLUSION

This study has not been concerned with whether prayer is of psychological benefit; it has made an attempt to uncover some of the problems inherent in the whole notion of petitionary prayer. In short, it has tried to discover whether petitionary prayer does anything more for the believer than self-suggestion would. Let us draw together the conclusions we have reached. First we saw that Jewish petitionary prayers must be understood as requests regardless of one's conception of God, and that they are of three sorts: (1) prayers for tangible objects; (2) prayers for a change in the psychological, physical, intellectual or religious welfare of an individual or a group; and (3) prayers for an event. We then saw that the difficulties connected with the notion of making a request to God are inherent in the concept of petitionary prayer and cannot be removed by an attempt to reduce prayers to expressions of faith in God, expressions of praise, and so forth. When one makes a prayer, we saw that if God is conceived anthropomorphically, making a request to Him is in many ways similar to making a request to another person. There would be no reason to assume that God could not be given new information by our prayers, or that He could not appear to us, reply verbally, or even explain the reasons for His decision to grant or not to grant our requests. But we should not expect God to give a verbal response or appear before us; nor should we always expect to know where God is, nor even expect Him to hear our requests and grant them. However if God is not at all like a human person, making a request to Him is radically different from making a request to someone. There is no reason whatsoever to assume that He would respond verbally to our requests, and we would be wrong to think He might appear before us or be informed by our petitions.

Furthermore if God is conceived anthropomorphically, there are numerous difficulties understanding how God grants prayers. In some cases - such as when God is asked to grant a tangible object - it is possible to have some idea how He could fulfill this request. But when it comes to understanding how God could grant a child, ignite a burnt offering, destroy a city or impart comfort, this is much more difficult to conceive. And when God is described as bringing about miracles, we are not only faced by these perplexities, but we also cannot be certain whether the alleged miracles actually took place. When we conceive of God as an incorporeal Being, these difficulties become even more serious - we could have no evidence that He had heard or granted our requests. Thus we could not be sure that we had experienced miraculous or non-miraculous divine interventions. And even if He did intervene, we would have no means of knowing it was really Him.

These observations lead to overwhelming difficulties concerning the efficacy of prayer. We saw that the principle that "God answers all prayers" is unassailable. There is no evidence in favour of it or against it. But there are important differences between this claim and the claim that "petitionary prayers are sometimes efficacious." Though people do not make this latter claim on the basis of scientific tests, they nevertheless believe in the efficacy of prayer on the basis of some kind of personal experience. Yet this marginal experimental basis does not constitute a sufficient condition for this claim to be true; rather it should be regarded as a necessary condition. Thus it seems impossible to convince someone else of the power of prayer; it is a conviction every person must come to for himself. In the debate between the believer and non-believer in the efficacy of prayer, there is no means of verifying or falsifying the assertion that petitionary prayers work. This same conclusion applies to prayers for God to give us guidance. Suppose we believe God tells us what to do and we feel that His advice is morally wrong, how can we know whether we should follow it or conclude that it was really of Divine origin. Even if we believe that God has given us advice of which we approve, our problems are not over; how can we be sure it is in fact from God? Suppose He is not a God who gives advice; imagine revelation is a non-propositional encounter with the Divine. Does it make sense then to ask him for help in the first place if there is such uncertainty about what He would want us to do?

Turning to a consideration of the acceptability of petitionary prayers, we saw that (with the exception of prayers for God to change the past which appear to be unacceptable in principle) the believer cannot know whether his prayers are acceptable. How can he determine whether they are for ends so trivial or unreasonable that they are of no avail? Even if they were shown to be offered thoughtlessly, maliciously or by a wicked individual, the prayers might be answered if God is more interested in what is being prayed for than in the frame of mind or character of the person who prays. Further the petitioner cannot know whether what he is praying for would be the right action for God considering its potential repercussions which only God could know and in the light of God's eternal plan. Finally when we turn to God's attributes as defined in the Jewish tradition, we are met with fearful problems. Even supposing that prayer does eradicate evil, how can we believe that an all-good and all-powerful God has permitted such evils to exist and constructed a process by which petitionary prayers can eliminate them? But if we assume that God is not all-good, or not all-powerful, or that evil does not exist, our difficulties increase. If evil is really an illusion, there is no point in praying for its eradication since it does not exist anyway. If God is not really all-good but all-powerful, there is no point in praying for the eradication of evil since God clearly does not want to eliminate it. But if God is not really all-powerful, but all-good, there seems to be no point in praying since God simply cannot eradicate evil even if He wanted to.

We are confronted with equally perplexing difficulties in considering God's omniscience and unchangeableness. If God is omniscient, it is <u>just</u> possible to believe in the efficacy of prayer, though this involves notions which are very difficult if not impossible to understand. The simplest and clearest explanation is that because of God's omniscience, petitionary prayers cannot possibly be efficacious. When it comes to unchangeableness, the problems are insurmountable. The presupposition behind petitionary prayer is that God can change the course of events as a result of prayer. Yet if a changeless God who is outside time does this, then He has to will two contradictory states of affairs simultaneously and eternally. Thus we can see that there is no conclusive evidence to prove that petitionary prayers have ever been answered. Furthermore, on the basis of an analysis of God's attributes as traditionally defined in Judaism, it seems impossible that they ever could be if God conforms to His traditional depiction.

To illustrate the implications of these conclusions, let us look at a concrete example of a prayer being offered to God. Imagine a crowded airport. Everyone is bustling about, some catching a plane, others waiting to meet family or friends. Suddenly there is an announcement: all the people waiting to meet a certain plane are told to go to a particular lounge for some important message. There is consternation; what can have happened? Then the news comes through: the airplane they were due to meet has crashed. There were two hundred people on board and apparently there are at least fifty, but no more than one hundred survivors. The only thing to do is to wait... and to pray. When the relations of all those passengers in the airplane were gathered together waiting for news, were they in any way helping their relatives through prayer?

Let us suppose that when the list of survivors is read out, one very pious lady exclaimed, "I knew my son would be spared. God always answers prayer." How could she make such a judgement? Presumably she has not interviewed every single occupant of that airport lounge to ask whether they were praying or not; it is hard to imagine that, having obtained this information, she correlated it with the names of those who survived. Presumably if there were no more than a hundred survivors, there must be some people there who had prayed for their relative or their friend, and that person had not survived. How could the pious lady explain this? No doubt if she had done some sort of statistical survey, and she had discovered that apart from her son all the other survivors had completely irreligious relatives, this still would not shake her belief that her son had been saved as a direct result of her prayers. She would no doubt be convinced to her dying day that her son's survival was entirely due to her activity at the airport and the fact that the other survivors had not been prayed for would remain a mystery for her.

Let us suppose that as a result of her statistical survey, she achieves the satisfactory result that only those passengers who have praying relatives have survived. This seems to be a clear victory for the supporters of prayer, but still there are problems. It seems totally unfair to those passengers who were alone in the world. Perhaps they were travelling to a foreign country and there was no one there to meet them. If God is all-good, it seems unfair that instead of sympathizing with their friendless state He merely causes them to be among the casualties because there was no one who knew about the accident who would pray for them. Perhaps on the airplane there was a very earnest, pious young Jew whose relatives were atheists and thus did not pray for him. How could God allow such a worthy young man to be struck down for his relatives' unbelief? The great likelihood however is that if someone tried to work out some sort of correlation between who prayed and who survived, they would discover that some survivors were prayed for and some were not; they would work out that among the dead, there were some with atheist and some with believing friends. What could be concluded from such an analysis? Those whose relatives had survived and who had themselves prayed would remain convinced that their prayers had made all the difference. Those whose relatives had died and who had not prayed would refuse to believe that prayer would have made any difference anyway. Clearly there can be no dialogue between those who believe in prayer and those who do not believe. Who knows if prayer does make a difference? Who knows whether a certain person's survival was the result of prayer or whether it was mere coincidence?

What would the pious lady feel if her son had not survived? She would no doubt think that God knew best, and that despite her prayers there was some reason that her son should not be among the hundred survivors. Perhaps she would feel that her son was "too good for this world." But if her son was so good that he died in order to have a superlative reward in the world to come, it is difficult to understand why his survival was prayed for in the first place. Perhaps on the other hand, the pious lady felt that her son had died because she herself had not offered sufficiently worthy prayers. She might well feel that her son's death was in some mysterious way a punishment from God for not being a sufficiently good person. Yet it is hard to believe this since surely if God is just, He does not allow someone to die because of someone else's misdeeds. Perhaps the woman could find no reason for her son's death, but she accounted for it by saying that as only a hundred people could survive, God knew that there were other people on board the airplane who were more worthy of being saved for one reason or another. But if God is all-powerful, He could surely have saved more people; no restriction was put on God as to the number of people He could have saved - He could easily have saved the lady's son if He had chosen to do so.

It might be however that she accounted for the failure of her prayer on different grounds altogether. She might say that she was really praying for herself, that she might have the strength to bear her son's death if that was what had happened. She might argue that she never believed that her prayer would in any way make it more likely that her son would be among the survivors. The airplane had crashed before the lady started to pray and it was the crash itself which determined who was to survive. Therefore when she started praying her son was already dead. But if this is what she really believed, why did she ever pray for her son's survival? The only prayer she could logically pray was "Oh God, if my son has died, help me bear it." The fact that she did not restrict herself to that one prayer indicated that in some mysterious way she did feel she was helping her son by praying for him.

Whether this lady's son survived or not, a large number of people died. The question we must ask is: how can God allow such an accident? God is supposed to be so good that He does not want air accidents and so powerful that He is able to know about them and to stop them. How can there be this terrible accident if God is really like this? Some philosophers might argue that the air accident was not really so terrible after all; that it was all part of God's eternal plan for His people and therefore good by definition. Anyone who had lost a friend or relative in the accident would find this point of view very hard to stomach. The commonsense view is that an airplane crash in which people are killed is an evil and that is the end of the matter. Yet even if this point of view were correct, it makes prayer useless; there is no point in praying to God to protect people who fly in airplanes if accidents are part of the divine plan and if it is God's will that they should occur.

Other theologians want to argue that aircrashes occur because God is not really omnipotent; aircrashes are beyond His control and although God wants to protect people who fly in aircraft, He is in fact unable to do so. Again this may well be the case, but if it is so then it is still useless to pray. If God is unable to stop aircrashes then there is no point in asking Him to do so. As a third alternative, it can be argued that although God is able to prevent accidents, He does not in fact wish to do so. This kind of God is different from the God in whom Jews have traditionally believed. Again there is no point in praying to this kind of God; He is most unlikely to be persuaded by our prayers if He positively wants aircraft accidents to happen. Anyway none of these solutions is satisfying to most believers. Our pious lady would want to say that God is all-knowing, all-powerful and all-good. Yet if He really has such a nature, then there would be no need for petitionary prayers in the first place since such things as aircraft accidents would surely not occur. Prayers to avert evil would be made redundant.

If the lady's son did die in the accident, she might well ask God for guidance. What should she do in her bereavement? It is difficult to know how she would expect God to answer this prayer; she would, no doubt, be highly surprised if she heard a great booming voice which said "Go to Miami Beach for a couple of weeks!" Firstly she would be unprepared to hear a voice at all and, secondly, the content of the message would be so astonishing to her that she would probably think that she had had an hallucination. In the Bible there are several instances of people hearing God's voice, but it does not seem to be a common phenomenon nowadays. Therefore when our lady prayed for revelation from God, she would expect "something to happen." If she arrived back home to find a letter from her nephew inviting her to spend a fortnight with him in Florida, she might regard it as an answer to prayer. On the other hand, when the rabbi telephoned her to ask if she would be the next chairman of the Sisterhood, she might feel that that was the answer to her prayer. But who is to say which was the true will of God? Perhaps He really wanted her to go to Miami beach; perhaps the Sisterhood idea did not come from Him at all. Perhaps He is not in favour of either idea and both invitations were complete coincidence.

Let us examine what kind of God the pious lady must believe in, if she believed that her prayers for her son could be fulfilled. Traditionally Jews have believed that God is all-powerful, all-good, and all-knowing. They believe that He is the Creator of the World and the great power behind it; presumably this is what our pious lady would believe. She would also believe that God, despite all these abstract attributes, would take a personal interest in her and in her affairs. We have already dealt with the difficulties involved in her believing that God fulfils petitions and in her believing that God is omnipotent and all-good. Yet she would also believe that God would be unchanging and omniscient. Presumably if her son died in the crash, she would believe that God knew it was going to happen in advance. If God is omniscient, He must know the future and thus - long before her son ever stepped on the airplane - He must have known his fate. He must also have known that our lady would pray for her son's life. The fact that He knew that she wanted her son to survive makes her prayer superfluous. There is no point in our lady explaining all the external circumstances of the crash since God must have already known them; there would be no point in her praying, since God would know what she was going to say before she articulated the words. In addition if God is unchangeable, He presumably does not change His mind. He knew about the son's death before it occurred and this knowledge does not change. If this is what God is like, how could the poor lady's request be granted?

Yet she might want to argue that although God knew that her son was going to die, He also knew that he would be prayed for. She might want to say that when God decided that her son would be killed in the accident, He also took the prayer into

account.   If she had not prayed, her son might have had an
even more painful death so in a sense her prayer "made a
difference."   Of course, she probably cannot know whether her
son's death was painful or not, that is a matter of faith.
Leaving that aside however if God is outside time – if He is
experiencing everything simultaneously and eternally – then
there was no moment of decision.   There was no time when God
did not know about the aircrash.   There was also no time when
God did not know about the prayer.   If this is the case then
the prayer made no difference.   Both the prayer and the crash
occurred as they did and they could not have occurred any
other way.   God knows what has happened, what is happening,
and what will happen, and He knows all these things all the
time.   He knows them correctly because He has perfect
knowledge and no prayer can change the course of that perfect
knowledge since God by definition knew about the prayer always
and does not change.   It seems that if the traditional picture of
God is correct, the poor lady's prayer for her son could not
have been efficacious.   Not only was it the case that it did not
work (but might have done given different circumstances); given
her definition of God, her prayer could never have been
efficacious.

But perhaps her idea of God was totally wrong.   Perhaps
God is not omnipotent, omniscient, all-good and unchanging.
Perhaps He is far more like a person than the traditional
picture led her to expect.   Certainly there are plenty of
instances in the Bible in which God seems to act in very much
the same way as a human being.   He changes His mind for
example, and He speaks.   If God is really like this, then there is
nothing inconsistent in our lady asking Him to save her son.   If
He had not been around when the accident occurred, He needed
to be given the necessary information and clearly prayer is the
mechanism set up to convey this kind of news.   No doubt if He
is a loving God (or, at any rate, as loving as any of the lady's

friends would have been), He would try to do the best He could. But since He is not all-powerful, it was not His fault that his efforts were not very successful. It might possibly be that this kind of God never even heard the prayer in the first place, since like a human being perhaps He can only be in one place at one time. Still, there is more hope that this lady's prayer would have been efficacious with this kind of God. At least it is worthwhile praying to such a God in the first place; unlike the traditional God, this finite kind of God could fulfill prayers. Unfortunately, given His limited nature, He may find it very difficult to do so.

In the Introduction, I said that there were three alternatives. We could conclude either that God can fulfill petitionary prayers and that He frequently does so; or we can conclude that although God can answer prayer, it is not in fact the case that He does. Then there is the third alternative- that God's nature is such that it is absurd to think that He ever could fulfill prayer. The picture of God cited in the most primitive passages of the Bible falls into one of the first two categories. It is not incongruous to think that the God who "walked in the garden in the cool of the day" (Gen. 3:8) would answer prayers if He could. However, we cannot know whether He does in fact answer them or not, and although some sort of probability could theoretically be worked through scientific experimentation, it is probably something human beings will never know for certain. However, as for the traditional Jewish concept of God, surely He must fall into the last category. Given that He is omniscient, omnipotent, all-good and unchanging, it is a mistake that our requests to Him could have any objective efficacy.

BIBLIOGRAPHY

Aquinas, St. Thomas: <u>Summa Theologica</u>, New York, McGraw Hill, 1963.

Augustine: <u>Works</u>, Edinburgh, T. and T. Clark, 1873.

Balme, H.: <u>The Relief of Pain: A Handbook of Modern Analgesia</u>, London, J.A. Churchill, Ltd., 1939.

Bevan, E.: <u>Symbolism and Belief</u>, London, Allen and Unwin, 1938.

Brunner, V.: <u>What Are We Doing When We Pray</u>, London, SCM Press, 1984.

<u>Daily Prayer Book</u>, New York, Hebrew Publishing Co., 1949.

Eichrodt, W.: <u>Old Testament Theology</u>, London, SCM Press, 1967.

Emmet, D.: <u>The Nature of Metaphysical Thinking</u>, London, Macmillan, 1945.

Ezra Ben Solomon: <u>Perush Al Shir Ha-Shirim</u>, Altona, 1764.

Farmer, H.H.: <u>The World and God</u>, London, Nisbet and Co. Ltd., 1935.

Flew, A. and MacIntyre, A. (Eds.): <u>New Essays in Philosophical Theology</u>, London, SCM Press, 1955.

Flew, A.: <u>God and Philosophy</u>, London, Hutchinson and Co., 1966.

Flew, A.: "Compatibilism, Free Will and God", <u>Philosophy</u>, 1973.

Geach, P.: <u>God and the Soul</u>, London, Routledge and Kegan Paul, 1969.

Hare, R.M.: <u>Applications of Moral Philosophy</u>, London, Macmillan, 1972.

Hebblethwaite, B>: "Some Reflections on Predestination, Providence and Divine Foreknowledge", <u>Religious Studies</u>, 15, 1979.

Heiler, F.: <u>Prayer</u>, London, Oxford University Press, 1932.

Hick, J.: <u>Evil and the God of Love</u>, New York, Harper and Row, 1966.

Hume, D.: <u>Dialogues Concerning Natural Religion</u>, New York and London, Hafner Publishing Co., 1969.

Hume, D.: <u>Enquiry Concerning Human Understanding</u> in <u>The</u>

English Philosophers from Bacon to Mill, New York, The Modern Library, 1939.

Idelsohn, A.Z.: **Jewish Liturgy**, New York, Schocken, 1967.

Jacobs, L.: **Jewish Prayer**, London, Jewish Chronicle Publications, 1955.

Jewish Encyclopaedia, New York, Funk and Wagnalls, 1901-1905.

Kretzman, N.: "Omniscience and Immutability", **The Journal of Philosophy**, July, 1966.

Leibniz, G.: **Theodicy**, London, Routledge and Kegan Paul, 1952.

Lewis, C.S.: **Miracles**, New York, Macmillan, 1971.

Lewis, H.D.: **Our Experience of God**, London, Allen and Unwin, 1959.

Lewis , H.D.: **Philosophy of Religion**, London, University Press Ltd., 1965.

Maimonides, **The Guide of the Perplexed**, New York, Hebrew Publishing Co., 1881.

Miles, T.R.: **Religion and the Scientific Outlook**, London, George Allen and Unwin, 1959.

Marmorstein, A.: **The Old Rabbinic Doctrine of God**, London, Oxford University Press, 1927.

Noth, M.: **Exodus**, London, SCM Press, 1962.

Petuchowski, J. (Ed.): **Understanding Jewish Prayer**, New York, Ktav, 1972.

Phillips, D.Z.: **The Concept of Miracle**, London, Routledge and Kegan Paul, 1965.

Pike, N. (Ed.): **God and Evil**, New Jersey, Prentice-Hall, 1964.

Pike, N.: **God and Timelessness**, London, Routledge and Kegan Paul, 1970.

Popper, K.: **The Logic of Scientific Discovery**, London, Hutchinson and Co., 1972.

Price, H.H.: **Essays in The Philosophy of Religion,**, Oxford, Clarendon Press, 1972.

Prior, A.: **Time and Tense**, Oxford, Clarendon Press, 1968.

Strawson, P. (Ed.): Studies in Philosophy of Thought and Action, London, O.U.P., 1968.

Stump, E.: "Petitionary Prayer", American Philosophical Quarterly, 16, 1979.

Swinburne, R.: The Concept of Miracle, London, Macmillan, 1970.

Swinburne, R.: "Omnipotence", American Philosophical Quarterly, July, 1973.

Von Rad, G.: Old Testament Theology, Edinburgh, Oliver and Boyd, 1962.

Wisdom, J.: Philosophy and Psychoanalysis, Beverley, University of California Press, 1953.

TORONTO STUDIES IN THEOLOGY